eco esca

United Kingdom

Green travel begins here...

ecoescape®

United Kingdom

written & edited by
Laura Burgess

GREENGUIDE

MARKHAM PUBLISHING • UNITED KINGDOM

Written & edited by Laura Burgess

Series art direction & cover design by Omaid Hiwaizi

ecoescape logo, responsible life cycle and maps designed by Eskimo Design (www.eskimodesign.org.uk)

Research by Laura Burgess, Gavin Markham, Freda Palmer, Victoria Peat and Catherine Mack

Cover image of Rhossili Bay, Swansea © britainonview/McCormick-McAdam (www.britainonview.com)
Unless otherwise indicated, or where images have been supplied by the businesses featured in
ecoescape, all original photos are copyright © Laura Burgess.

The ecoescape logo is a registered trade mark

First edition published April 2007 by Yellow Room Publishing
This edition published March 2008 by Markham Publishing

ISBN 978-1-905731-40-4
Text copyright © 2008 Laura Burgess
Design copyright © Markham Publishing

Markham Publishing
31 Regal Road, Weasenham Lane Industrial Estate, Wisbech,
Cambridgeshire PE13 2RQ
United Kingdom
T: +44 (0) 1945 461 452
E: distribution@markhampublishing.co.uk
www.markhampublishing.co.uk

Printed and bound in the UK on FSC-certified, sustainable paper and board by Cambrian Printers Ltd,
Llanbadarn Road, Aberystwyth, Ceredigion SY23 3TN
T: +44 (0) 1970 613 000 E: info@cambrian-printers.co.uk W: www.cambrian-printers.co.uk

The views expressed in this guide are not necessarily those of the publishers.

Although we have tried to ensure the accuracy of the information provided in this book, the publishers
are not liable for any inaccuracies or inconvenience arising thereof.

Contents

ecoescape – the journey to here...

If I stopped to think about what I was doing two years back, I may never have embarked on the journey that became ecoescape. But I'm glad I did. I had no idea if ecoescape could survive beyond the first edition I self-published in 2007. If you've already come across ecoescape before picking this book up, then thank you, your interest and support has made this journey possible.

The first ecoescape book was well-loved, well-understood and well-read. It was also an experiment into lots of unknowns. It might not always have gone quite to plan but I learnt a lot along the way. Most importantly, the purpose I set out with achieved its aims which were to provide people with ideas of green places to stay and visit along with things to do in the UK. ecoescape aims to encourage a rediscovery of landscape, attractions, foods and dwellings closer to home. It promotes alternatives to flying to encourage travellers to tread gently as they go. I continue to be overwhelmed when I hear people's stories of their own ecoescapes and about new and existing businesses that are doing their bit to support environmentally friendlier tourism.

And so here we are in 2008. This time ecoescape has been made possible after a chance encounter I had at the London Book Fair last year. I met Gavin, the publisher, who believed

in ecoescape and said he wanted to publish it. So now we are
author, publisher and reader, at the first of an exciting new
series of guides that will continue to spread ecoescape's
message. We hope to contribute to the growing awareness
about the environmental effects of travelling. We feel
ecoescape is already a part of this shift and will continue
to turn up the volume of people who believe in responsible
escapism. I hope you enjoy reading ecoescape and
more importantly that it is a guiding force for planning
time away.

So with ecoescape in hand, head and heart we hope you look
forward to adventures and escapes that you may or may not
have thought possible in the UK and beyond. And don't
forget ecoescape is about more than what we have to say.
It is about a dialogue, or an eco-logue as we call it. All the
businesses in ecoescape rely on your feedback. That's why
we'd like you to tell us about your travels. We've created a
website at www.ecoescape.org with a view to it becoming
a visitors' book where you can share your thoughts with
others interested in developing responsible escapism
in the UK and beyond. So it's over to you to carry on
the story-telling... ■

Laura Burgess
March 2008

www.ecoescape.org

Sunset at Thetford Forest © Julian Claxton

Responsible escapism

Is this the end of no-frills travel? Has our love affair with cheap travel finally nose-dived into the ground? And how can we look for travel experiences closer to home that don't cost the planet and offer what we always wanted – some escapism?

Two years ago I found myself thinking about how travellers needed something new. The type of escapism offered by many travel companies seemed uninspiring, needless to say costly in terms of the environment. So as I began to ponder this issue I came up with a philosophy. No – I don't mean logic problems or the meaning of life, but a simple love of thinking about what travel is and what it could be for myself and others. This led me, with a little help from Proust, to set up ecoescape with the mission of helping travellers to see the world with new eyes and discover the true meaning of responsible escapism.

ecoescape doesn't help time-pressed travellers to see more of the world and achieve that '100 places to visit before you die' thing. Nor do we promote eco-destinations in far flung places. Instead ecoescape helps people lessen their impact on the planet by finding ways to get off-grid using sustainable transport, slow food and more natural daily rhythms closer to home in the UK and around. For some people this might be more of a change than for others. This is why ecoescape is all about nurturing a new mindset about what travel is and how we travel through time and space in the world. We don't dictate a set of dos and don'ts. Instead we aim to create inlets to finding a greener holiday based on things we all like to do and experience already.

We research and visit the ecoescapes to ensure they will help reduce your impact on the environment and offer a real sense of escaping the daily grind. So while we recognise that some businesses have invested more time and money into sustainability than others, we want you to be a part of deciding how green it is. This is why we're creating a two-way dialogue so you can tell the business owners how they're doing and share your stories with other travellers.

The next few pages will explore what an ecoescape is. It's not a science, although there are a lot of eco-friendly alternative technologies at play behind the scenes; instead our aim is to inspire you to set off on new paths to responsible escapism. ■

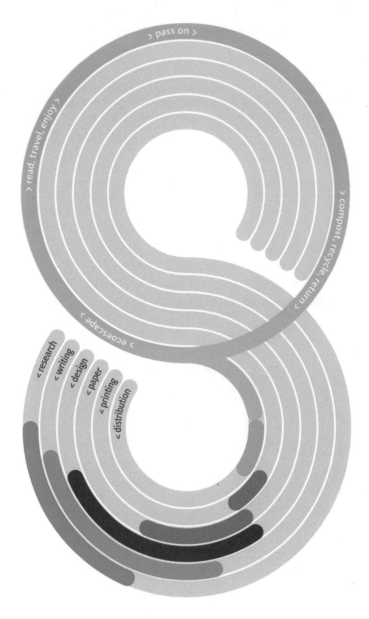

> pass on >

> read, travel, enjoy >

> compost, recycle, return >

< ecoescape <

< research
< writing
< design
< paper
< printing
< distribution

ecoescape's responsible life cycle

The responsible life cycle

For ecoescape, the medium really is the message. Like most people we're not perfect but we try to keep the responsible life cycle (left) at the centre of everything we do, ensuring the book and our business tread as carefully as you do.

The responsible life cycle is a way of recognising that our actions, no matter how big or small, have an impact on the environment. When we put together the first edition of ecoescape, we knew that along with a message to help travellers go green, it was crucial to be respectful of the resources we needed to produce a guidebook. We've continued this mantra into the production of this book and subsequent editions in the series. In the responsible life cycle, the reader also takes responsibility for the impact of the guide through recycling, sharing and composting. And so the cycle continues.

The responsible life cycle is also a metaphor. It helps keep our travels grounded because it reminds us that travel is about the impact of an entire trip. That means from our home, through a journey to a destination and back home again. ecoescape not only offers inspiration but also encourages you to share your stories of responsible escapism. People have been sharing stories about travel since prehistory. Storytelling has helped humans survive, protect and enjoy their environment and that's why we hope you will feel inspired to share your experiences with others at **www.ecoescape.org**.

How did we make this book?

Research: We hopped on trains, buses, bicycles, bio-taxis and, of course, used our legs. See our Slow Travel Tool Kit on page 127 for our advice on how to get around the UK without a car or plane.

Energy: website and computers powered by the wind see **www.green-hosting.co.uk** and **www.ecotricity.co.uk**

Print: We use Cambrian Printers in Aberystwyth, Wales. They have won numerous awards for their green printing, collect water from the roof for their presses, only use FSC-certified papers and boards and even have a wormery under the stairs for their organic waste. Using a UK printer means it costs us more than going overseas but then we think profit is measured in more ways than the pennies in our pocket. The book is printed on 100% recycled paper using vegetable-based inks. ■

The Boggles' House at Bewilderwood in Norfolk (see page 64-65)

Getting off-grid: home

'Home is where one starts from.' TS Eliot

You may wonder why we talk about home in a guide that's about travel and getting away. ecoescape begins at home. It's about reconnecting to familiar places – our cities, villages, birthplace or countries – and finding ways to escape that we may never have realised were there.

We also want you to discover new spaces to think and breathe. ecoescape helps you find ways to get off-grid at home and further afield without sacrificing the quality of travel experience or the potential to relax and escape everyday life.

We think of an ecoescape as our getting-off-grid way of being. Whether you see home as something that is (pretty much) fixed, a metaphor or even a transitional place to lay your head and stash your belongings, home is a space for dwelling and disconnecting from the stresses of life and work. Often this is an idea, not a reality. This means finding ways to escape are important, if not essential! We call this process getting 'off-grid', both mentally and physically in a way that also reduces the impact of our travels on the environment. That's why our ecoescape suggestions are forms of responsible escapism; they minimise the impact on the planet's resources and offer a more sustainable approach to getting-off-grid when we travel. From experience we know that when we then return home we feel more inspired to integrate sustainable ways of living into our everyday lives.

We think that the greenest travel options for ecoescaping are on our doorstep not only because we'll be reducing our carbon emissions by travelling closer to home but also because the choice for green places to stay and visit in the UK is growing by the day. The recommendations in ecoescape take into account the environmental cost of our travel bug and are real ways to reduce the impact we have on the environment. ■

Getting there slowly:
the journey

We need the earth to see the earth. No matter how hard we try, we'll never separate the environment from travel. It is at the centre of every trip we make. It gives us the energy to reach our destination, however near or far and often we get the desire to travel in order to experience a different environment.

But how much longer can we afford to neglect thinking about the transition that takes us from A and B? It's often the part of the holiday we least look forward to. In fact we've also become adept at maximising our distance and minimising the costs of travelling. By doing so, we've developed an ostrich-like approach in ignoring the effects of travel. We make excuses for taking flights when a train could suffice. We tell ourselves one journey won't matter as we jump in the car when walking could be possible. If we were to look at the journey before deciding on the destination, just think how different our experiences would be and how much easier it is to take the environment into consideration.

Slow travellers are now rekindling a sense of adventure in an always-on, globally interconnected and 'I can get (pretty much) anywhere on the planet within 24 hours' kind of world. The boundaries of slow travel are being explored by those avoiding airports and motorways.

Travelling slowly overland anywhere in the world is becoming a way of harnessing the journey so that what we see on the way is as important as what we do when we arrive. And that's why you'll find details of public transport and ways to arrive at the ecoescape destinations without using a car or a plane. As we've tried and tested many of these ideas, we're able to prove that it's possible.

We know that ecoescaping will take some people a while to understand. But with gradual changes we think it is possible to introduce new ways of thinking about travel that will lead to long-lasting lifestyle changes. There would be no sense in creating a guide that tried to save you time and money while promoting the needs of

Help for slow travellers

The Slow Travel Manifesto:
www.slowtravelmanifesto.org

Indispensable guide to public transport in the UK:
www.transportdirect.info

Book your train tickets:
www.thetrainline.com

Plan your cycle routes:
www.sustrans.org

Turn to page 127 to consult our Slow Travel Tool Kit for more advice and slow travel tips.

the environment and planet. You see, our journey isn't necessarily about distance. Nor is it just about time. It's about adjusting our mindset that connects our way of thinking about travel to how we move through time and space.

When we've dealt with these questions, suddenly the desire to squeeze ourselves onto a 1p flight to 'save' time, or tick off 'must-see' boxes declines. In doing so we have found people come to think of how their lives are a part of a bigger story we are all writing about and how our actions (big and small) ripple outward. ecoescape is all about making these ripples happen by ensuring our journeys have a positive impact. ■

Rhossilli Bay near Swansea © britainonview/McCormick-McAdam

Dad with friends enjoying some slow travel and responsible escapism

Private troubles and public issues

The easiest way to become a responsible escaper is to start with what you know and love. This is at the heart of ecoescape's philosophy and part of our way of creating 'inlets' to finding our 'ecoescape island'. So if your passion is the great outdoors, ecoescape can help you to find a way to get outside while exploring green places to stay and visit along the way.

In the case of my father, he was a keen mountain biker long before the green credentials of cycling were recognised. He just liked to escape to the mountains of the Lake District and has always been respectful of the environment he needs for his sport. So you see ecoescaping was not difficult for him and he now uses his ecoescape guide to help find campsites and B&Bs that promote green travel.

We hope that you, the reader, will find an aspect of this book that you can connect to. Perhaps it will be the prospect of a wildlife encounter, a fabulous restaurant or an opportunity to take the children out for the day. Or perhaps you've been on several holidays in the past that are better for the environment and you'd like some more inspiration. We're certain you'll find it in this book.

None of us can solve the world's troubles alone. Nor is it realistic to expect individuals to suddenly change their lifestyles. This is made even worse if we are unsure that our elected leaders and governments aren't playing their part in making tough decisions about public transport, climate change or protecting our natural environment. But if individuals don't connect to these public issues, it's unlikely things will improve.

Travel is just one area which has long put pressure on the environment and ecoescape is helping people think about the challenge to change. Like we said we don't have a set of rules or formulas but we do provide alternatives that we believe are contributing to making green travel more rewarding, comfortable and fulfilling both in the short and the long-term. ■

'Private troubles and public issues' from C. Wright Mills.

How green do we go?

One of the most frequently asked questions is 'how does ecoescape decide which businesses to include in the book?' The next few pages will explore the thinking behind what we include in our guides.

None of the businesses have paid to be included in the book. Nor do we get paid commission for every holiday you book using ecoescape. We keep our editorial decisions independent from commercial ones. Although many of the businesses have received formal awards for their green initiatives, ecoescape has another set of requirements which are difficult to measure. We look for businesses that demonstrate that along with fulfilling the criteria set by green accreditation schemes and government initiatives, they offer innovative ways of involving their customers in the travel experience. The business owners need to offer guests an insight into the local communities that sustain them through their supplies of energy, food, drink, local crafts and expertise. We include eco-awards such as the green leaf of the Green Tourism Business Scheme (see left) as an additional guiding point for readers.

An ecoescape is about what the destination offers as an experience and a way to get 'off-grid'. In other words the business has to add to the stock of stories about responsible escapism. The ecoescape suggestions in this guide therefore contribute to a storybook of how the owners think travel is possible whilst also paying respect to the natural environment in which they live and welcome others to stay.

We've also found that businesses do not adopt a like-for-like approach to sustainability. By the very nature of sustainability, business owners find that they have to adapt to their surroundings to ensure their patch of the environment is protected. This could be looking out for the local wildlife or using a renewable natural resource to generate energy. So the businesses featured in this book each have a story that connects the founders' biographies and the direction of their

Helpful links

 Look out for the leaf of the Green Tourism Business Scheme (pictured). This shows that a business has achieved a gold, silver or bronze award according to the level of their environmental performance. For further information about the accreditation scheme running throughout the UK, visit **www.green-business.co.uk**

Other schemes in the UK

Peak District Environmental Quality Mark:
www.peakdistrict.gov.uk/eqm

Welsh Green Dragon awards:
www.greendragonems.com

New Forest Green Leaf Tourism Scheme:
www.thenewforest.co.uk

Green Island Tourism for the Isle of Wight:
www.greenislandtourism.org

business to the local environments they have chosen to inhabit, protect and invite others to experience.

ecoescape uses four main criteria to map how a business in the tourism industry reduces its impact on the environment. These are: conservation, energy, waste and food.

Under these headings there are numerous ways a business can improve its environmental performance. All of the business owners in ecoescape take each area seriously and they'll opt for various ways to deal with these areas, carefully using, renewing or micro-generating resources obtainable in a specific location. Of course there is a lot of variation too. Some business owners might grow their own produce; generate energy through solar panels; encourage use of public transport, offer an honesty shop, or invest in ingenious ways of recycling waste.

Once we're convinced that all measures possible are taken by the business owners we want to make sure the experiences they offer are attractive. This doesn't necessarily mean that every room should have a widescreen TV, tea-making facilities or a trouser press. We look for places and destinations that not only have a strong environmental commitment but incorporate all their responsible escapism credentials into an experience that shouldn't put customers off. After all, no one likes being preached to, especially when they are on holiday. ■

Hadrian's Wall in Northumberland © britainonview/Rod Edwards

Case study: Pinetrees, Suffolk

Pinetrees in Beccles opened its doors in 2005. Sue and Graham, the owners, went on a journey of their own to realise their dream of creating a sustainably-built and managed bed and breakfast. Here we map out their journey and show some of the highlights along the way.

- Founders, Sue and Graham, work for sustainable transport charity and bank

- Keen cyclists with a dream to build an eco B&B in the UK

- Spend many years looking for the right plot and environment

- Find plot in the outskirts of Beccles in Norfolk

- Hire local architect to realise their eco-dream

- Start building using sustainably sourced timber

- Introduced rain harvesting for toilet flushing and clothes washing

- Created bio-system to treat sewage

- Nurtured wild flower meadow around the property

- Created natural habitats including tree planting

- Developed small holding with hens, fig plants and vegetable plot

- Introduced recycling and towel policy

- Link up to Sustrans national cycle route

To read more about Pinetrees, turn to page 68.

How green do you go?

ecoescape will never compromise on comfort or quality of escapism. Of course luxury is a question of taste and for some people it might mean spending the weekend doing what they love doing like surfing or simply relaxing with friends and family and eating good food. An ecoescape business must facilitate the everyday things we already love doing together with environmentally friendly infrastructures and activities that compliment, but tend not to become the foreground of a travel experience. We promote quality experiences at the centre of every ecoescape.

Under the Thatch © Kiran Ridley

Now tell your story

Don't forget that the strength of the force to bring about changes to the way we travel is partly reliant on you telling your stories of responsible escapism to others. So please visit our website at **www.ecoescape.org** and tell the businesses, other escapers and us what you think about our selection. You can always contact us with your own ecoescapes as well.

Our email address is **tellyourstory@ecoescape.org** ■

From station to nation

ecoescape partner Virgin Trains tell us how they are encouraging people to explore the UK by train.

Here's the thing. Sometimes we all feel guilty about travelling these days, because we know there's a cost to the world we love. But it doesn't have to be like that. Some forms of travel are less harmful to the environment than others, and some are really rather friendly. For example, did you know that travelling by one of Virgin Train's Pendolinos emits 76% less CO_2 than an equivalent journey made by plane or car? Which means that you get to see new places and faces with none of the downsides. That's exactly what makes working with ecoescape so brilliant. It inspires us all to have the time of our lives without damaging the planet while we do it. The guide and website have the low-down on everything green – from activities, to holidays, to places to eat. The only question is how are you going to get to enjoy them all?

That is, of course, where we come in with dozens of stations, for you to choose from, on our network. And it needn't cost the earth to see the world, in more ways than one. Our Value Advance fares mean that if you book ahead you'll make huge savings, particularly if you're flexible on your times and can travel off-peak. There are loads of Value Advance fares available every weekday, so it should never be a problem to get hold of a couple. The great thing too is that if you travel by Virgin Trains the journey itself becomes part of the fun – play a game, read a book, listen to music – and just let the world slip by. So why not make guilt trips a thing of the past and get out and about on Virgin Trains? You know it makes sense.

Green light for Virgin Trains
We don't just talk the talk:

- We have committed to serving fairtrade hot drinks onboard and in all our First Class lounges
- We've launched Europe's first 20% bio-diesel train
- We use recycled or sustainable office paper, and actively reduce paper use
- Our earth-safe drivers are trained in the latest energy saving driving techniques.

- We recycle old mobile phones and printer cartridges, raising money for charity.
- As part of Envirowise 'Big Splash' campaign, we're monitoring and cutting back water usage at stations
- With the help of Envirowise and Rail Gourmet, we keep our onboard product packaging to a minimum

To check out our commitment to the planet, or to book your Value Advance ticket online, just visit: **www.virgintrains.com**

50 of the UK's best ecoescapes

The South West

Scotland

The North
of England

The Midlands

East Anglia

Wales

The South East
& London

The South West

The South East & London

East Anglia

The Midlands

The North of England

Wales

Scotland

St Ives is fast becoming one of my favourite places in the UK. It's got so much going for it that I decided to include two in-depth features for places to stay in St Ives in this edition. The first is Primrose Valley Hotel. This is one to savour and digest like a fine wine. The hotel is a second from the sandy Porthminster Beach and when it opened in 2001, the nouveau chic followed.

With the double whammy of being green, this is an inspirational find. Andrew, one of the partners in the hotel believes that going green is about taking small, but positive steps in the right direction. His guests are gently coerced into more sustainable living through small actions. The do-not disturb sign, reads, 'shhh. I'm relaxing' but cleverly reminds his guests about the huge impact of simply turning off the lights when leaving a room. He also champions a visitor payback scheme to raise money for the Marine Conservation Society, for which the hotel has become a platinum supporter.

The staff carry out regular green meetings to ensure that they are on course to sustainability. A host of Cornish suppliers keep the restaurant stocked up: try Ernie's butter, John's cheese, Norma's marmalade and Nigel's mackerel for authentic Cornish flavours. When Andrew realised that the fish for the fish pies came from an unsustainable source, he scrapped it from the menu and now ensures that all the fish is line caught and from sustainable stocks. He also encourages his guest to arrive by public transport and suggests 50 things to do without the car in Cornwall on the hotel's website.

t: +44 (0)1736 794 939
w: www.primroseonline.co.uk

Contact details

Address: Porthminster Beach,
St Ives, Cornwall TR26 2ED
Telephone: +44 (0) 1736 794 939
Website: www.primroseonline.co.uk
Price: £100-£145 for a double room;
suite £175-£225
Opening times: Open all year except
December-January
Disabled access: There is no
disabled access

Getting there slowly

Take the train from Truro to St Erth
and then hop on the coastal line to St
Ives. There are also regular buses to
the town from Truro and Penzance. As
space is scarce in this little town
driving can be troublesome.

Visit the Tate Gallery

A visit to St Ives isn't complete with-
out a wander around the Tate Gallery. The modernist building overlooks
Porthmeor Beach and sits amid alleyways of artist studios. The café is a perfect
spot to enjoy the views to sea and try some local Cornish produce.
Address: Porthmeor Beach, St Ives, Cornwall, TR26 1TG
Telephone: +44 (0) 1736 796226
Website: www.tate.org.uk/stives

Eat at Porthminster Beach Café

While you're lying on the stunning Porthminster beach, wafts of good cuisine
drift along the sand from the beachside Porthminster Café. The café specialises
in local seafood and sources its vegetables from its very own kitchen garden.
Even if it's just a good cup of tea you're after, the café is open all day for after-
noon tea on the terrace as well as light lunches and evening meals.
Address: Porthminster, St. Ives, Cornwall TR26 2EB
Telephone: +44 (0) 1736 795 352
Website: www.porthminstercafe.co.uk

The Vyvyan family has been resident at the Trelowarren Estate for over six centuries. Keen to re-establish the estate as a self-sufficient community with a healthy work force, the present owner, Sir Ferrers, has tirelessly brought it back to life with ecologically sound timeshare properties. His feudal approach to the rejuvenation of the estate is all about longevity and the future of the land beyond his lifetime using techniques of the past to achieve this.

Not surprisingly the woodland surrounding the properties is the lifeblood of the estate providing fuel for the impressive seven-tonne biomass boiler. The trees are sustainably coppiced to produce the fuel – a medieval forestry technique that increases sunlight and promotes biodiversity in the woodland. The heating from the boiler is then piped to the holiday accommodation, restaurant and leisure centre with its outdoor chemical-free swimming pool. Rainwater is also harvested for eco dishwaters and washing machines.

The wood clad properties are available as a time-share or when they're not occupied, as self-catering holiday rentals. This ensures that occupancy is sustained throughout the year and local employment is supported. Trelowarren's award winning New Yard Restaurant is supplied with organic pickings from the estate including wild garlic and fresh mint. The present Vyvyan family will also leave their mark on the estate's history through their 350-year tree planting scheme consisting of a lime avenue and an area laid out with 160 oak trees set in an 18th Century grid formation.

t: +44 (0) 1326 222 105
w: www.trelowarren.com

Contact details
Address: Mawgan, Helston, Cornwall TR12 6AF
Telephone: +44 (0) 1326 222 105
Website: www.trelowarren.com
Price: A week's self-catering holiday in one of the properties costs between £450 and £2650 depending on the size and season
Opening times: Year round
Disabled access: There are two properties that have disabled access – Gweal Gullas and Penhillick

Getting there slowly
It's difficult to reach Trelowarren without a car, but there are buses to the nearby villages of Goonhilly and Helston (nearest rail link is Redruth). From Goonhilly, it's about a 20-minute walk.

Eat at the Green House
Although Trelowarren's restaurant has earned itself an enviable reputation, the nearby Green House offers a super alternative. A quiet, friendly young couple run the restaurant preparing and serving delicious meals made from local organic produce. They've created a cosy atmosphere which feels as if you're dining in their home.
Address: 6 High street, St Keverne, Helston, Cornwall TR12 1NN
Telephone: +44 (0) 1326 280 800
Website: www.thegreenhouse-stkeverne.co.uk

Orchard Lodge perches on top of the hill overlooking Boscastle Harbour – the location of the catastrophic 2004 flood. The town has bounced back and now there's a visitor centre chronicling the events of August 2004. Further up the hill Orchard Lodge is set back from the tourist trail in relative tranquillity. The north Cornish coast is only 10 minutes walk away and provides some panoramic views and delicious sunsets.

Newcomers to the B&B trade, Shelley and Geoff, began their new life in Cornwall in 2006. The renovation of the white house has given over to a modern, fresh look. The rooms contain souvenirs of the couple's travels abroad along with inspiring Thomas Hardy quotations on the walls. Shelley and Geoff collect eggs from a local farm, one of the few local ingredients that's not delivered to their door. Everything else, from smoked kippers to organic milk, arrives fresh and ready for breakfast.

As one would expect with a name like Orchard Lodge, there is an abundance of fruit in the garden, primarily apples and pears. Timing my stay to perfection, the apples were dripping off the trees and every now and then a thud signalled another had landed. Those that weren't munched straight from the tree formed the staple ingredient in Geoff's breakfast Autumn compote – a warming mix of spices and fruit. Orchard Lodge has an expanding eco-policy in operation including efficient appliances and central heating, along with recycling facilities and discounts for those arriving by public transport. They are members of the Cornwall Wildlife Trust and Shelley has completed a qualification in sustainable tourism.

t: +44 (0) 1840 250 418
w: www.orchardlodgeboscastle.co.uk

Contact details

Address: Gunpool Lane, Boscastle, Cornwall PL35 0AT
Telephone: +44 (0) 1840 250 418
Website: www.orchardlodgeboscastle.co.uk
Price: £27-£37 per person per night
Opening times: All year, except closed for 2 weeks from December 20th to January 5th
Disabled access: There are no ground floor bedrooms, but some rooms have 10 steps to climb

Getting there slowly

A direct bus service (the Western Greyhound number 594) runs from Bude to Truro stopping at Boscastle en route. You can also connect to Bodmin Parkway Station via Wadebridge. If you travel from Wadebridge or Truro, make sure you alight at the stop on Doctor's Hill before the descent into Boscastle Harbour or it's a steep walk back up the hill.

Visit the British Cycling Museum

The bus between Boscastle and Wadebridge passes the eccentric Bicycle Museum. Hop off the bus and enjoy a nostalgic insight into bicycles, past and present. Each bicycle tells a different story and owners John and Sue are all too willing to tell you about each frame, lamp and piece of memorabilia. The museum is open year round, Sundays to Thursdays.
Address: The Old Station, Camelford, Cornwall PL32 9TZ
Telephone: +44 (0) 1840 212 811
Website: www.chycor.co.uk/cycling-museum

Eat at the Napoleon Inn

I opted for some good quality pub grub at the Napoleon Inn – only a minute's walk from Orchard Lodge. The real ales served straight from the barrel are tremendous and come from down the road in St Austell. The pub dates back to 1549 and has beautiful old slate floors and oak beams.
Address: High Street, Boscastle, Cornwall PL35 0BD
Telephone: +44 (0) 1840 250 204
Website: www.staustellbrewery.co.uk

A side step off the Camel Trail, Cornish Yurt Holidays is tucked away on the edge of Bodmin Moor. With wild scrubland to the south, and valley views to the north, you'll wonder when to expect Ghenghis Khan over the hillside. Cornish Yurt Holidays is as close to Mongolia as you'll get in the UK. Tim, the owner and expert in yurt construction, creates an authentic and sustainable camping experience for his guests. He has recently started running courses in a variety of rural craft and bushcraft skills. These include cooking over open fires, wild food cookery and fire craft. The aim is to give guests a close to nature experience when they stay and some new campcraft skills to go with it.

The wood he uses to build the yurts is from local sources, some from his own land, and is coated with natural non-toxic preservatives and oils. This embalms the yurts in a soft calming essence, particularly in the special bathroom yurt. Here the roll-top bath beneath the stars is an experience to savour. The wood burning stove (hand-built in Devon) heats the water and on a dark night with the lanterns lit, the bathroom turns into paradise. The two richly decorated sleeping yurts cater for four to six people comfortably. The set-up is ideal for lounging around on super size cushions next to the warmth of the wood burner. The yurts are completely off-grid and meals are enjoyed by the light of the lanterns. Tim is happy to supply his guests with local organic produce and eggs laid by his hens. There is also a micro yurt for the composting toilet with a painted floor and comfy beech seat.

t: +44 (0) 1208 850 670
w: www.yurtworks.co.uk

Contact details
Address: Greyhayes, St Breward, Bodmin, Cornwall PL30 4LP
Telephone: +44 (0) 1 208 850 670
Website: www.yurtworks.co.uk
Price: £295-£450 per week (up to 6 people), short breaks are also possible
Opening times: March-October.
Disabled access: There is no disabled access as the yurts are situated at the bottom of a hill only accessible by a narrow winding path

Getting there slowly
The village of St Breward isn't served very well by public transport. You can either take a taxi from Bodmin Parkway Station or even better bring your bicycle and cycle along the Camel Trail – a mainly flat, shaded route through woodland.

Eat at the Potters Barn
At the nearest point on the Camel Trail to Cornish Yurt Holidays, the Potters Barn offers tea, coffee and lunches to thirsty cyclists and walkers. You can try local cheese and Cornish apple juice in the impressive converted barn. Open Tuesday to Sunday, the Barn also offers cycle hire.
Address: Wenford Bridge, St Breward, Bodmin, Cornwall PL30 3PN
Telephone: +44 (0) 1 208 850 471
Website: www.thepottersbarn.com

Making Waves is a bright and cheerful self-catering appartment close to the harbour at St Ives. When Simon, the owner, ran a guesthouse from here, he built a reputation for serving up the best vegan breakfast in St Ives. As it turned out, I was one of the last guests to sample his vegan bangers and I'm certain they'll be missed by his regular guests. In 2008, however, Simon is concentrating on welcoming guests to his self-catering appartment and perhaps he'll pass on a tip or two about vegan sausages that hold together in the pan.

Simon spends much of the winter months gathering driftwood and reclaiming materials for his interior design projects, like the reclaimed timber table, once part of the St Ives fishing industry. You can see the results of his craftsmanship in the house which is full of his work. The bathroom at the top of the stairs is a treat and contains a stylish cast iron roll-top bath. The Suma toiletries in the rooms compliment the chemical-free environment and come in cute paper packets. There are no TVs here, just peace and quiet and shelves full of books to read on the rare occasions that the sun doesn't shine in St Ives. Otherwise, bring your paintbrush and easel and join the artists that congregate on this stretch of coast. However, watch out for the mischievous seagulls, which have been swiping ice creams and pasties from the hands of unsuspecting tourists. Brandished as thieves, the locals have started a campaign against feeding them. However, all you really need to do is exercise a bit of care when slurping your lolly.

t: +44 (0) 1736 793 895
w: www.veganholiday.co.uk

Contact details
Address: 3 Richmond Place,
St Ives, Cornwall TR26 1JN
Telephone: +44 (0) 1736 793 895
Website: www.veganholiday.co.uk
Price: Self-catering appartment
sleeping 2-4 £350-£695 per week
depending on the season
Opening times: Year round
Disabled access: There is no disabled
access

Getting there slowly
You really should travel by train to St
Ives. Not only is it far easier than arriv-
ing by car, but the coastal rail route is
an excellent prologue to your escape.
The London to Penzance line stops in
St Erth where you can connect to serv-
ices to St Ives.

Eat at Blas Burgerworks
Not your usual burger joint. These tasty patties, both meaty and vegetarian, are
all cooked with local ingredients. The beef is naturally reared and free range. The
restaurant has a strict recycling policy and composts much of its waste. The
atmosphere is relaxed and informal as diners gather round reclaimed timber
tables. For vegetarians, the sunflower burger is a definite hit.
Address: The Warren, St Ives, Cornwall TR26 2EA
Telephone: +44 (0) 1736 797 272
Website: www.blasburgerworks.co.uk

A stalwart supporter of sustainable tourism in Cornwall, Gill of Bedknobs, is leading the way on keeping things green for her guests. Preferring the role of caretakers than proprietors of the old Victorian mansion, Gill and her partner Kim are taking on a slow but sustainable restoration project. They're currently overseeing the facelift of the crumbling conservatory using the existing cast-iron frames to restore the windows to their former glory. In fact all the work at Bedknobs is based on sustainability and not short-term savings.

The snug rooms are heated using an energy efficient gas boiler and solar panelling takes care of the hot water. The garden surrounding the house is full of intrigue, offering clues to its past including the remains of an old glasshouse and a rebuilt section of wall hidden in the trees. This was once the entry point for two sisters to reach each other between neighbouring gardens. The rooms are furnished with antique pieces and lush quilts. In the bathroom you'll find organic and chemical-free toiletries, all of which have been part of Gill's long-term research project to find high standard environmentally friendly suppliers.

In a similar vein, the breakfast menu is propped up by a list of local suppliers sourced through Plough To Plate – a Cornish trade supplier. So you'll find Davey's Cracking Good Eggs, honey from the Lost Gardens of Heligan and butter from the Trewithen Dairy. The Cornish porridge with brown sugar and clotted cream is a personal recommendation.

t: +44 (0) 1208 77553
w: www.bedknobs.co.uk

Contact details
Address: Polgwyn, Castle Street, Bodmin, Cornwall PL31 2DX
Telephone: +44 (0) 1208 77553
Website: www.bedknobs.co.uk
Price: From £65 for a double room and £50 for single occupancy
Opening times: Year round
Disabled access: There are no ground floor rooms but assistance is offered to help the less abled to climb the stairs. Handrails are present in each of the bathrooms

Getting there slowly
You can catch direct trains from London to Bodmin Parkway railway station. If you're arriving from the north, Cross Country Trains run services via Birmingham, Bristol and Exeter to the South West. From Bodmin Parkway station, the Western Greyhound bus number 555 (direction Padstow), run hourly services to Bodmin Town. Otherwise if you bring your bicycle, the railway station is located on the national cycle network route 33 which passes through Bodmin town.

Visit the Eden Project
If you've not yet visited the Eden Project, try avoiding the crowds outside of the summer season. You'll be assured of a more relaxed visit around the mighty biomes and even more so if you leave the car at home. There are regular shuttle bus connections to the site from St Austell railway station. Cyclists also receive discounts on the entry price.
Address: Bodelva, Cornwall PL24 2SG
Telephone: +44 (0) 1726 811 911
Website: www.edenproject.com

Forget everything you know about surfing. Visualise some eco-chic comfort along with tailor-made surfing lessons to help you progress on the waves. This is the offering of Ed and Mod, the brains behind Global Boarders. They wanted to offer would-be surfers the opportunity to learn the sport without harming the environment or compromising luxury. And so slick sustainable surfing was born.

You can choose from different vacation packages depending on time, accommodation and ability. Many of the participants are beginners but generally by the end of a week's surfing you'll be able to catch a green wave – an unbroken wave and trickier than the white water equivalent. But the best part of Global Boarders is the fact that you'll have the opportunity to travel to the best surf spots during your stay as the instructors keep both ears to the ground, or sea, to ensure optimum surfing and the best waves. It's a different approach to the more usual surf and get smashed tradition in Newquay and means that participants can get to know the different beaches and landscapes of Cornwall.

Global Boarders now has three luxury barn conversions where guests can stay before being taken out to the sea for the day's surfing. The barns are all low energy and contain hefty recycling facilities. Guests are also escorted to local restaurants in the evenings to sample some local flavours. Ed is adamant that, despite common misconceptions, the seawater around Cornwall is clean and even clear in places. And as a sponsor of the successful campaign, Surfers Against Sewage, Global Boarders is certainly playing a role in keeping it that way.

t: 0845 330 9303
w: www.globalboarders.com

Contact details
Address: Lowena, Chynoweth Lane,
St Hilary, Penzance,
Cornwall TR20 9DU
Telephone: 0845 330 9303
Website: www.globalboarders.com
Price: A City Slicker weekend break
(two nights) costs from £305 per per-
son including surf lessons and B&B
Opening times: Year round
Disabled access: Disabilities can be
catered for in the accommodation, but it's advisable to phone ahead to find
out more

Getting there slowly
The majority of participants arrive by train and there are regular direct services
from London to Penzance. You can save time and take the overnight sleeper
service and arrive ready to take on the waves in the morning.

Eat at Salt
If you take part in a holiday organised by Global Boarders, you'll be introduced to
a number of good local eateries. Salt is one option. It's a café and bar serving
local and fresh produce. There are some hot chunky sandwiches on the menu
along with big platters of cheese and meats to share. During certain evenings,
live bands entertain the diners.
Address: Ground Floor, White's Warehouse, 25 Foundry Square, Hayle,
Cornwall TR27 4HH
Telephone: +44 (0) 1736 755 862
Website: www.salt-hayle.co.uk

Devon's answer to Bambi, Tarka the Otter is the hero of the long acclaimed children's book by Henry Williamson. Although the story is over 80 years old, it continues to inspire walkers and cyclists to explore the unchanged landscapes of North Devon meticulously described in Williamson's book. The Tarka Trail cuts a path through Williamson's country and is over 180 miles in length following part of the Devon Coast-to-Coast route. At Braunton cyclists can set out on a 32-mile easy ride to Meeth in the south following a reclaimed railway track. The path is level, well-surfaced and traffic-free. Since the trail has been part of a long-term sustainable tourism project, it has benefited from ongoing management to allow the wildlife on the embankments and verges to flourish. One scenic stretch of the route follows the banks of the River Taw. Although sightings of otters are rare, it's easy to imagine how the story of Tarka emerged from the waters where the fictional otter began his journey to sea. The route is also mapped out with waymarkers, audio posts and sculptures to help cyclists and walkers to get to know the area better. Hiring bikes is also easy at various points en route. At Barnstaple there's an ideal opportunity to pick up a hire bicycle from Bike Trail at the railway station. From there on enjoy the scenic views and picture-perfect Devonshire villages.

t: 0870 608 5531
w: www.tarka-country.co.uk

Contact details
Address: The cycling trail starts in Braunton, travels through Barnstaple and ends in Meeth
Telephone: 0870 608 5531 (the Discover Devon Holiday Line and see also www.discoverdevon.com)
Website: www.tarka-country.co.uk; www.sustrans.org.uk; www.biketrail.co.uk
Disabled access: Some cycle hire shops provide bicycles for disabled people to use on the trail

Getting there slowly
Depending on where you start on the trail, there is usually somewhere to arrive by public transport. Take the Tarka Line from Exeter to Barnstaple with or without bicycles. See www.carfreedaysout.com/tarka for more details.

Eat and stay at Yarde Café
On the Tarka Trail at East Yarde, you'll stumble upon the Yarde Café, an organic eatery famous for keeping trail users fed and watered. The little café has a composting toilet and reed bed system as part of its efforts to maintain its small section of the Tarka countryside. David, the owner has also recently opened an eco-friendly bunkhouse next to the café.
Address: Yarde Café, East Yarde, Near Torrington

'Uncle Bob', the founding father of Churchwood Valley left a legacy ensuring that the Churchwood Valley holiday park remained respectful to the natural environment. Today the site has grown modestly in size in keeping with the conservationist's wishes. John and Shirley, the present owners, have worked hard to win their David Bellamy Gold award every year for 12 years running. The professor himself was so impressed with the park that he vowed to support the ongoing development at Churchwood Valley.

The wooden cabins have become a part of the natural environment. They were built using chestnut for cladding, Monterey pine for fences and elm for internal cladding – all grown, planked and seasoned on the Churchwood estate. The sheer leafiness of the park drapes each cabin in a green cascade from where you can enjoy a privileged window on the wildlife. The natural habitats in the park have been so well looked after that the cabins are great places to view up to 100 species of bird.

Each cabin also has its own private clearing surrounded by trees and shrubs – perfect for al fresco dining. There's an onsite shop for some essentials and a recycling centre which copes with just about every type of rubbish. The tree trimmers and strimmers generate piles of cuttings which are turned into compost giving vitality to the flowers and shrubbery which are also fed using conserved rainwater. Wembury beach is a short walk away where you can try a rockpool ramble when the tide is out. John has dreams of creating a woodland nature trail on the estate but for now is happy with his occupation of selling 'peace and quiet' to his guests.

t: +44 (0) 1752 862 382
w: www.churchwoodvalley.com

Contact details
Address: Wembury Bay,
Plymouth, Devon PL9 0DZ
Telephone: +44 (0) 1752 862 382
Website: www.churchwoodvalley.com
Price: Prices range from £245-£825
for a week's stay in a cabin
Opening times: 19th March 2008-
15th January 2009
Disabled access: One of the newer
cabins is fully accessible to wheelchair users and has a shower in the bath and
some other cabins are offered as 'easy access'

Getting there slowly
Catch the number 48 bus from Plymouth (Viaduct). FirstBus runs hourly services
to Wembury from Monday to Saturday. Alight at the Odd Wheel pub and
Churchwood Valley is a 15 minute walk along a road through woodland.

Visit the Marine Centre at Wembury
Learn more about the marine wildlife at the Marine Centre by the beach in
Wembury Bay. Admission is free to the centre which closes during the winter
months. You can explore the rocky reefs and find out why this part of the coast-
line is part of a Site of Special Scientific Interest.
Address: Church Road, Wembury, Plymouth, Devon PL9 0HP
Telephone: +44 (0) 1752 862 538
Website: www.wemburymarinecentre.org

Eat at Langdon Court Hotel
The splendid Langdon Court Hotel is a five minute walk through the woods from
Churchwood Valley. Langdon's restaurant uses fresh local seafood, organically
reared meat, game and local garden produce.
Address: Down Thomas, Plymouth, Devon PL9 0DY
Telephone: +44 (0) 1752 862 358
Website: www.langdoncourt.com

Mill on the Brue is all about children. A visit to this activity hub is likely to remain engrained in their memories right into adulthood. Perhaps it is the morning spent pressing apple juice, or the afternoon on the riverside assault course. Mill on the Brue re-introduces children to the outdoors and connects the countryside to their everyday lives. Part of their job during a stay is to help tend and harvest vegetables from the kitchen garden. Being only metres from their plates, suddenly carrots and chard take on a whole new meaning. The same goes for some of the meat they eat which comes from the animals reared on the farm. Matt, one of the directors of the centre, takes the view that the children are better off being told the fate of the farm pigs, Wallace and Gromit. So the children leave the centre with a healthy appetite and a better understanding of the traceability of food.

Mill on the Brue has invested in sustainable technology and given Matt some interesting projects to explore like his homemade solar panels for the newly built drying room. For the more ambitious jobs like the Long House, however, he has enlisted the help of a local architect who used a sustainable approach for the construction of the Mill's main building. With panoramic views over the river, the building not only caters for herds of children, but also wedding receptions. A large trench was dug under the ground to feed the geothermic heating system for the Long House and the soil extracted went into building Matt's snake mound. The slates on the roof are made from recycled rubber tyres and the walls are insulated with sheep's wool and warmcell. Rainwater is harvested for the loos and all the wood for the construction came from four miles up the road.

t: +44 (0) 1749 812 307
w: www.millonthebrue.co.uk

Contact details
Address: Trendle Farm, Bruton, Somerset BA10 0BA
Telephone: +44 (0) 1749 812 307
Website: www.millonthebrue.co.uk
Price: Prices vary depending on the group size
Opening times: Year round
Disabled access: The Long House has disabled access, but some of the other areas on the site require step or slope access

Getting there slowly

Bruton's railway station has direct trains from Bath and Bristol. Otherwise Castle Cary railway station (direct trains with London Paddington) is a taxi ride away. The centre encourages arriving by public transport and even sends a member of staff to accompany children from London.

Stay at Gant's Mill

If bunkbeds and tents should be left for the kids, then Gant's Mill is an ideal alternative. It's even accessible along the grounds of Mill on the Brue where the river divides and powers the hydro electric turbine at Gant's Mill. The turbine provides more than enough electricity for the bed and breakfast and even makes a tidy profit from the National Grid. The accommodation is comfortable and the food is mainly local. Brian and Alison also welcome visitors to wander around their manicured gardens.
Address: Bruton, Somerset BA10 0DB
Telephone: +44 (0) 1749 812 393
Website: www.gantsmill.co.uk

Eat at Truffles

Produce from Mill on the Brue hasn't far to go and much of it ends up on the plates at Truffles, just around the corner. The menu here is entirely dependant on what the locals can supply and don't be surprised to see customers pop by with a bag of damsons, or whatever else they have harvested that day. The restaurant is also handily located along the fish run to Bath and Bristol from the south coast and so has a regular supply of seafood and fish. The only ingredient sourced from outside the West Country is duck which travels from Suffolk. The friendly young husband and wife team that run the restaurant are adamant that local food is the back bone of their business and is what keeps the menu fresh and the food tasty.
Address: 95 The High Street, Bruton, Somerset, BA10 0AR
Telephone: +44 (0) 1749 812255
Website: www.trufflesbruton.co.uk

Andreas Von Einsiedel

Fashionable Clerkenwell is home to a fashionable hotel, the Zetter. It's got all the modern gadgetry – think i-pod decks and free WiFi, along with unexpected, but cool extras like wool-covered hot water bottles and swipe card vending machines distributing champagne and toothbrushes. The décor mixes retro with city style, and the rooms, although some quite small, speak good taste and thoughtful design.

Leaving the latest trends aside, the Zetter has been doing well at greening its business. The hotel is in a converted warehouse and uses FSC-certified timber from sustainable sources. It is independent of mains water as the supply comes from deep below the ground via the hotel's own pump and borehole. There is individually controlled air-conditioning in all 59 rooms of the hotel and the public areas but what makes this special is that it is also retrieved from the borehole. Additionally the building is ventilated naturally by skylights in the central glass atrium when the sun comes out. Recycling goes on here along with energy saving timers for light bulbs. The restaurant on the ground floor serves Mediterranean-influenced dishes which change with the seasons. There's an extensive wine list and an eclectic mix of cocktails featuring real fruit served in the 70s-inspired bar area.

t: +44 (0) 20 7324 4444
w: www.thezetter.com

Contact details

Address: St John's Square, 86-88 Clerkenwell Road, London EC1M 5RJ
Telephone: +44 (0) 20 7324 4444
Website: www.thezetter.com
Price: Double rooms start at £160 plus VAT per night
Opening times: Year round
Disabled access: There is a lift to the rooms, and some are adapted for disabled travellers

Getting there slowly

The Zetter is a short walk from Farringdon tube station. The nearest national railway station is King's Cross.

Eat at Water House Restaurant

From the people who opened Acorn House (see page 49), Water House goes even further into self-sufficiency and carbon savings. The restaurant uses a heat pump connected to nearby Regent's Canal to provide a cooling and heating system. A solar thermal installation on the roof heats the water and Water House saves its waste water for use in its own community garden created out of its composted organic food. The menu is organic, fresh and seasonal.
Address: 10 Orsman Road, London N1 5QJ
Telephone: +44 (0) 20 7033 0123
Website:
www.waterhouserestaurant.co.uk

Edmund Sumner

Andreas Von Einsiedel

Approaching their city habitat much like Londoners, the nesting birds at the London Wetland Centre appear to tolerate life beneath one of the world's busiest flight paths. In fact, the wildlife and birds thrive in what used to be a series of redundant reservoirs. The Wildfowl & Wetlands Trust transformed the area into 30 lakes, ponds and marshes with over 200,000 water plants and 27,000 trees. The Trust ensures that wildlife functions as a community and is in constant check of the delicate balance of species. This, of course, does not exclude humans, who are encouraged to observe and explore but respect the harmony of the wetland. Life in the wetlands is examined in finer detail through the exhibits and interactive discovery centre. The arrivals lounge at the 'bird airport' is a unique glass observatory where visitors can view the flocks of international birdlife.

The reedbeds on the wetland are a vital part of the natural eco-system. They clean incoming water by filtering any harmful solids. As well as being home to rare species of birds, they also play an important role in wetland industry by providing reeds for thatched roofs and bedding for livestock. Visitors can bring their binoculars and make the most of the purpose-built hides scattered around the site. Elsewhere there is a sustainable garden to help you green your own backyard through water conservation, recycled containers and careful selection of plants. The garden also offers alternatives to peat-based garden compost which has endangered the peat bog wetlands in the UK and abroad.

t: +44 (0) 20 8409 4400
w: www.wwt.org.uk/london

Contact details

Address: WWT London Wetland
Centre, Queen Elizabeth's Walk,
Barnes London SW13 9WT
Telephone: +44 (0) 20 8409 4400
Website: www.wwt.org.uk/london
Price: With Gift Aid, entry costs £8.95
for adults and £4.95 for children (aged
4-16). A family ticket is £25 and
concessions get in for £6.70
Opening times: Summer (March-
October): 9.30am to 6pm
Winter (November-February):
9.30am to 5pm

Disabled access: There is very good disabled access at the centre. The grounds
have level access and hard-surfaced paths with tarmac on the main routes.
There are also low-level viewing windows in the bird hides

Getting there slowly

From Hammersmith tube station, follow signs to the bus station. Take bus number
283 from Stand K which transports you directly to the centre. Alternatively buses
33, 72 and 209 stop nearby (alight at the Red Lion stop, approximately 150 metres
walk from the wetland centre).

Stay at Apex City Hotel

Located at the heart of London's financial district, the Apex City of London Hotel
proves that environmental concern is best for the bottom line. This recent modern build incorporates a string of environmentally friendly design features. The
rooms are flawless without being corporate and many enjoy views of Tower
Bridge. The hotel group has also developed an impressive set of operational
standards to reduce, reuse and recycle. Staff share ownership of these policies
including ethical purchasing and greener communication channels.
Address: No 1 Seething Lane, London EC3N 4AX
Telephone: +44 (0) 20 7702 2020
Website: www.apexhotels.co.uk

Eat at Acorn House Restaurant

Acorn House opened in 2006 amid claims to be the UK's restaurant to focus on
sustainable principles and training young would-be chefs. The restaurant director and head chef have combined their long and inspiring culinary careers with
the potential to make a real difference in the promotion of healthy eating,
reduction of waste and championing British produce.
Address: 69 Swinton Street, London WC1X 9NT
Telephone: +44 (0) 20 7812 1842
Website: www.acornhouserestaurant.com

The farm at Beachy Head has taken diversification to some imaginative ends. My favourite is the onsite micro brewery housed in an old farm building. It supplies guests and locals with the Beachy Head Original Ale produced using English hops in the most sustainable way possible. Charlie will be more than happy to supply you with a bottle or two during your stay.

The cottages are an alluring trio of converted farm buildings retaining their original features with long views over the fields out to the south coast. Guests are supplied with organic meat from the farm along with other local produce from the village market. Recycling bins are provided for most waste and green waste is fed to the chickens in return for freshly laid eggs. The added insulation of the cottages keeps off the winter chill and ensures the buildings are as energy efficient as possible.

Guests and children in particular will love the Sheep and Countryside Centres on the estate which provide a hands-on experience of the local wildlife and history of the area. The Seven Sisters Sheep Centre has one of the largest collections of rare sheep in the world with over 40 different breeds in residence. Hiker's Rest coffee shop offers exactly that, so wearied walkers can stop for tea and homemade treats. There are also suggestions for walks that start and end here taking in the dramatic white cliff faces of Beachy Head.

t: +44 (0) 1323 423 878
w: www.beachyhead.org.uk

Contact details
Address: The Dipperays, Upper Street, East Dean, East Sussex BN20 0BS
Telephone: +44 (0) 1323 423 878
Website: www.beachyhead.org.uk
Price: The cottages range from £395 per week in low season to £950 in high season for the largest cottages sleeping six people
Opening times: Year round
Disabled access: One of the cottages, Chestnut Lodge, has disabled access

Getting there slowly
There is a regular bus service run by the Brighton Bus Company between East-bourne and Brighton which stops at East Dean a short walk from Beachy Head.

Eat at the Tiger Inn
Also on the Gilbert estate, the Tiger Inn serves up the farm's meat produce and ales, along with an ever changing menu built on local availability. The pub is full of character with its beamed ceiling and history of smuggling and shipwreck.
Address: The Green, East Dean, East Sussex BN20 ODA
Telephone: +44 (0) 1323 423 209
Website: www.beachyhead.org.uk

This eco-lodge is tucked away in a secluded spot on the edge of the Pevensey Levels. Its cosiness means that staying in is just as much an option as taking to the outdoors. The lodge is decorated in natural pine with white walls and modern clean furniture throughout. The building opens onto a covered veranda overlooking the organic garden – a perfect spot to while away the hours come rain or shine. The lodge is south east facing, catching the warmth and light of the morning sunshine allowing you to enjoy your cornflakes and croissants al fresco. Heat is retained inside the building through solar efficient glass for windows. The lodge is built using wood from sustainable woodland in the UK and insulated with recycled telephone directories and newspapers. Guests are also encouraged to recycle and leave the car at home. There's plenty to explore on foot in the low lying Pevensey Levels which is a Site of Special Scientific Interest. The wide angle views are dominated by reclaimed wetland areas and push out to the South Downs just a few miles from the coast. This means that wildlife thrives in the area so birdwatchers are advised not to forget their binoculars.

t: +44 (0) 1323 844 690
w: www.littlemarshfoot.co.uk

Contact details

Address: Mill Road, Hailsham,
East Sussex BN27 2SJ
Telephone: +44 (0) 1323 844 690
Website: www.littlemarshfoot.co.uk
Price: Prices start at £400 for a week
long break (sleeps up to four people).
There are also short break offers from
October-March
Opening times: Year round
Disabled access: There are two steps
to the main entrance but the ground
floor is level throughout

Getting there slowly

The nearest railway station is Polegate
which has direct links with London Victoria, Brighton and Eastbourne. There
are regular buses from Polegate that
travel to Hailsham where it's a short
walk to Little Marsh Foot.

Visit Middle Farm

Nearby lying at the foot of the South
Downs is Middle Farm. Sixth generation
farmers run the 625-acre farm and are

passionate about good quality British produce achieved through respecting the
environment and looking after the animals. Visitors can see the working farm in
action and meet the friendly chickens, ducks, spotted pigs and donkeys. The farm
shops and restaurant serve every imaginable type of British food and drink available including the UK's National Collection of Cider and Perry featuring the farm's
own Pookhill Cider.

Address: Middle Farm, Firle, Lewes, East Sussex BN8 6LJ
Telephone: +44 (0) 1323 811 411
Website: www.middlefarm.com

Paskins Townhouse makes the term 'boutique' seem redundant. This hotel near to the seaside puts as much emphasis on its levels of comfort and design as its unique angle on hotel design. Its non-conformism inspires and delights its guests who'd rather hark back to the pier and promenade past than look for the town's nightlife. Or if they do, they may take tea first. The reception area frames the hotel's Art Nouveau leanings with its black iron-work contrasting with the yellow splashed walls and bold portraits. There are 19 further insights into the owners' distinctive taste in the individually appointed rooms and the pièce de résistance – the Art Deco breakfast room.

Understandably the people of Paskins want to make a big deal of breakfast. Not only for its unique setting, but also its delicious food – well worth the unexpected wake-up call in the morning. The breakfast menu is local, organic and fairtrade including both oak-smoked bacon from Old Spot Farm in Piltdown and homemade herby vegetarian sausages. The speciality Pavilion Rarebit is a dish to be admired for its eccentricity and proves itself as a fine competitor for the Full English. All this can be washed down with an array of fruit juices and freshly ground fairtrade coffee. The rest of the hotel follows strict environmental standards including organic toiletries in the bathroom and numerous energy saving initiatives.

t: +44 (0) 1273 601 203
w: www.paskins.co.uk

Contact details
Address: 18/19 Charlotte Street, Brighton BN2 1AG
Telephone: +44 (0) 1273 601 203
Website: www.paskins.co.uk
Price: Singles cost from £45 and doubles £85
Opening times: Year round
Disabled access: There is no access for people in wheelchairs but the hotel caters for other disabilities

Getting there slowly
Paskins is about a mile from the main railway station in Brighton. You can walk it in about 20 minutes or a little more if you stroll along the promenade. There are regular direct trains to Brighton from London taking about 50 minutes.

If Paskins is full...
stay at Brighton House

Let's face it; at certain times of the year, tourists arrive in droves to Brighton. So if Paskins is full, try the slightly more economical, but equally environmentally-sound option of Brighton House further along the promenade. You'll find an organic breakfast, and tastefully decorated rooms. The owners have become adept at saving energy and have even installed an insulating sedum roof.
Address: 52 Regency Square, Brighton BN1 2FF
Telephone: +44 (0) 1273 323 282
Website: www.brighton-house.co.uk

Eat at Terre à Terre
Terre à Terre takes creative cuisine to a whole new level. And there's not a scrap of meat in sight. The vegetarian dishes more than live up to their intriguing menu titles like Miso Pretty being an Asian sushi mix. My favourite was Poke Mole and Turtle Soup – another meat-free explosion of flavours consisting of sweet potato fritters, avocado mousse, lime oil and warm spice corn. Much of the food and drink is organic including some local brews of lager and cider.
Address: 71 East Street, Brighton BN1 1HQ
Telephone: +44 (0) 1273 729 051
Website: www.terreaterre.co.uk

When Brenley Farm hit difficult times, the Berrys opened their impressive house up to guests. And when the guests arrived, Maggie liked nothing more than to serve food from their farm or from farms nearby in Kent. This means that the breakfast choices regularly change but whatever you go for, it's always exquisitely prepared doing excellent justice to the producers themselves. Try some toasted muffin with rocket, poached egg and hollandaise or crispy bacon from a nearby farm.

Brenley is still a working farm – the grounds are lined with apple and pear orchards as well as a small acreage of hops which help supply the local Shepherd Neame brewery. The rooms are spacious and immaculately presented with luxury toiletries and fairtrade teas. The Berrys are big animal lovers so don't be surprised if the odd cat sneaks into the room.

Outside the house, the farm nurtures its diverse wildlife, from foxes to owls to bats. There is also an abundance of wild flowers and hedgerows with berries. Near to the entrance of the farm is a converted Georgian stable building used as a bunkhouse to accommodate up to 24 people with facilities for cooking. You can even bring your horse for a weekend away as there are special 'B&B' facilities for your equine companions.

t: +44 (0) 1227 751 203
w: www.brenley-farm.co.uk

Contact details
Address: Brenley Lane, Boughton, Faversham Kent ME13 9LY
Telephone: +44 (0) 1227 751 203
Website: www.brenley-farm.co.uk
Price: £70-£80 per night per room (double)
Opening times: Year round
Disabled access: There are stairs to the bedrooms and the front door

Getting there slowly
Brenley Farm is midway between Faversham and Selling railway stations. There are direct trains from London Victoria. It is a three-mile walk to Brenley Farm from the station or else taxis are usually available.

Visit Brogdale Horticultural Trust
Brodgale is home of the National Fruit Collection, a natural gallery of colour and taste and responsible for preserving the genetic diversity of England's cultivated fruit. The Apple Collection is thought to be the largest in the world and incorporates both new and established varieties, some dating back to the reign of Henry VIII.
Address: Brogdale Road, Faversham, Kent ME13 8XZ
Telephone: +44 (0) 1795 535 286
Website: www.brogdale.org

Visit the Shepherd Neame Brewery
Once you've seen the hops, you'll need to taste the brew. Before tracking down a local pub, visit the ale at source for a brewery tour in Faversham. Shepherd Neame is Britain's oldest brewer and has been a pillar in the Faversham community since 1698. The tour takes in the market town as well as a tasting session.
Address: 11 Court Street, Faversham, Kent ME13 7AX
Telephone: +44 (0) 1795 532 206
Website: www.shepherd-neame.co.uk

Kent Downs Area of Outstanding Natural Beauty

A rainy day in the Kent Downs wasn't enough to put us off a bracing December walk along the Pilgrims' Way. In fact, Derek and his dog like nothing better than grey skies and downpours: 'no such thing as bad weather for walking', he says to me over his shoulder. I was yet to be convinced as I lost my hopelessly inadequate trainer shoe to the mud. However, as the trail opened up in front of us and Derek brought to life tales of pilgrims' journeys, the magic of the Kent Downs soon reached me.

By the end of our long walk, it was clear why Derek decided to start a walking company that followed the glorious Pilgrims' Way. Derek's walking routes don't necessarily have to be accompanied by a guide. He'll happily meet you at the railway station and send you off with map, itinerary, packed lunch of local produce and directions on how to drink your weight in ale as you go. His insight and local knowledge make a Walk Awhile tour an excellent way to find out how Kent became the 'garden of England'.

Derek will even make sure your luggage arrives ahead of you at your B&B or hotel. His accommodation options are never faceless chains – he hand picks the best local B&Bs that offer a further taste of Kent's produce. Incredibly, nearly all of his customers arrive by public transport. Although the pilgrims wouldn't have had the luxury of train travel, walkers today can make easy connections with London by rail to Rochester and Canterbury – the start and end of the walk.

t: +44 (0) 1227 752 762
w: www.walkawhile.co.uk

Leeds Castle in Kent – see www.britainonview.com

Contact details
Address: Montgreenan, St Catherine's Drive, Faversham, Kent ME13 8QL
Telephone: +44 (0) 1227 752 762
Website: www.walkawhile.co.uk
Price: Two night self-led tours start at £208 per person. Guided tours cost from £304.
Opening times: Year round
Disabled access: Disabled access is limited on the walks as the trails go through fields and rough ground

Getting there slowly
Usually pre-arranged with Derek, but Rochester and Canterbury railway stations are good places to start and end a tour.

www.britainonview.com

Eat at the Woolpack Inn
One option of many, the Woolpack Inn offers a welcoming open fire to toast your cold toes or otherwise quench your thirst. The food is also seasonal and delicious. The Woolpack Inn is located in the quaint village of Chilham, on the Pilgrims Way and offers a host of Shepherd Neame ales.
Address: Chilham, Nr. Canterbury, Kent CT4 8DL
Telephone: +44 (0) 1227 730 351
Website: www.woolpackchilham.co.uk

If sleeping in a converted chapel isn't enlightening enough, then staying in one of the UK's greenest B&Bs is bound to get you thinking. Old Chapel Forge has acquired countless awards and green celebrity status for its dedication to reducing the impact of every aspect of its business. There's solar panelling to heat the water along with measures like grey water recycling and providing food produced by local farmers. All waste wood ends up in the wood burner and junk mail becomes fire lighters.

The history of the house and chapel dates as far back as 1611 and the site became one of 82 landing grounds during the Second World War to which Clarke Gable was one of its famous visitors. Today the chapel rooms offer uncontested luxury with high beamed ceilings and wrought iron fittings, made by the owner himself. There are luxurious natural toiletries in the bathroom – even sun lotion for sun seekers as well as additive-free refreshments for the children. The breakfasts are impressive and coupled with Sandra's hospitality, it'll become your favourite part of the day. For healthy eaters, platters of fruit are on the menu, or otherwise expect a full English of organic local produce. Chichester Cathedral is just down the road, as well as the more fast-paced action at Goodwood Racecourse.

t: +44 (0) 1243 264 380
w: www.oldchapelforge.co.uk

Contact details

Address: Lagness, Chichester, West Sussex PO20 1LR
Telephone: +44 (0) 1243 264380
Website: www.oldchapelforge.co.uk
Price: Rooms start at £50 per couple and include breakfast
Opening times: Year round.
Disabled access: All chapel rooms are on the ground floor

Getting there slowly

Bognor and Chichester railway stations are closest to Old Chapel Forge. You can arrange a pick-up with the owner or walk the two miles or hail a taxi.

Eat at the Dining Room at Purchase's

If you venture into Chichester city centre, try the Dining Room for well cooked and imaginative dishes. Located in the mansion of the country's oldest wine merchants, the Dining Room specialises in seafood and runs an extensive environmental policy.
Address: 31 North Street, Chichester, West Sussex PO19 1LY
Telephone: +44 (0) 1243 537 352
Website: www.thediningroom.biz

britainonview/Simon Kreitem

Without a doubt, the best way to experience the countryside is on foot or by bicycle. A holiday by bicycle gives you all the freedom you need and you can, of course, avoid traffic and congestion. Country Lanes has established itself in two of England's national parks – the Lake District and the New Forest – to offer travellers a range of cycling holidays and cycle hire facilities. The best part about it is that you can hop off the train at Windermere in the Lake District or Brockenhurst in the New Forest and pick up your bicycle from the hire centres nearby. In fact, the Brockenhurst outlet is housed in a restored railway carriage next to the station platform.

Both centres have facilities for children offering trailers and smaller bicycles to hire. There are themed rides to choose from as well as connections to the Isle of Wight from Brockenhurst so you can cycle to the ferry and do a spot of island hopping. You can choose a self-guided holiday or one of the Country Lanes guides can take you out for the day or longer. At each location the friendly and knowledgeable staff will help you find the best routes according to ability and terrain. There are over 100 miles of Forestry Commission off-road tracks to explore. The network links the main New Forest villages with the railway station at Brockenhurst by the safest and most attractive routes. From Brockenhurst you're likely to encounter forest donkeys, ponies and cattle, which like to wander between trees and occasionally visit the village itself.

t: +44 (0) 1590 622 627
w: www.countrylanes.co.uk

Contact details
Address: The Railway Station, Brockenhurst, Hampshire SO42 7TW
Telephone: +44 (0) 1590 622 627
Website: www.countrylanes.co.uk
Price: Adult cycle hire starts at £14 per person per day
Opening times: January-November

Getting there slowly
This is a fine example of a slow holiday. Arrive by train at Brockenhurst. There are direct connections with London which is a 90-minute journey. For more information about going green in the New Forest visit www.thenewforest.co.uk.

Stay at Sandy Balls
Families on bicycles will love Sandy Balls in the New Forest. Here you can stay in lodges nestled in 120 acres of woodland. The site has a prestigious David Bellamy Gold Conservation Award to its name and provides a number of nature walks for its guests. There's also a solar heated swimming pool, electric site vehicles and waste segregation initiatives.
Address: Godshill, Fordingbridge, Hampshire SP6 2JZ
Telephone: +44 (0) 1425 653 042
Website: www.sandy-balls.co.uk

britainonview/Martin Brent

S Fossey

The fictional world of Boggles and Twiggles comes to life at the boutique theme park Bewilderwood. The story follows the adventure of Swampy, a young Marsh Boggle who uncovers the mystery of Scaaaaary Lake. Visitors to Bewilderwood can follow in his footsteps, book in hand, and discover shoe-stealing Thornyclod spiders and dancing wood Twiggles. That's if you make it past Mildred, the Crocklebog lurking beneath Scary Lake. The founder and author, Tom Blofeld, unleashed his imagination and opened up a whole new world for his guests, young and old alike. 'This is the deli of theme parks,' he told me 'and we want parents to enjoy it with their children.' So expect grown adults to hurtle through the canopy or come screaming down Slippery Slope slides.

And Tom's fictional world is sustainable. Located in the heart of the Norfolk Broads, the marshland, reeds and woods are a perfect setting for an eco-theme park. Bewilderwood fits into its location as though it's been there forever. Visitors are requested not to upset the Twiggles by dropping litter or harming the wildlife and the wood used for the tree houses comes from a sustainable source. The vessels that transport visitors along the Dismal Dyke are recycled lifeboats and practically silent as they travel through the green algae-topped river. The barbeque sends a waft of irresistible cooking around the place and if a Twiggle burger isn't your thing, there's plenty of other locally-sourced fare on offer. Bewilderwood's founders have a long list of plans to put into action including taking the site off-grid, offering tree house accommodation as well as creating new sites around the country.

t: +44 (0) 1603 783 900
w: www.bewilderwood.co.uk

Contact details

Address: Horning Road, Hoveton, Wroxham, Norwich NR12 8JW
Telephone: +44 (0) 1603 783 900
Website: www.bewilderwood.co.uk
Price: entry costs £10 (under three go free) and 3 & 4-year-olds £5. A family ticket for up to six people is £45 (£7.50 per additional person)
Opening times: 17 March-7th September 10am-5.30pm; 8th September-2nd November 10am-4.30pm
Disabled access: Certain areas might be tricky for disabled visitors, but where possible ground walkways are even for wheelchair access and there are disabled toilets

Getting there slowly

From Norwich take the train to Hoveton station, 20 minutes away. There is a 45-minute walk from the station (turn right out of the car park and follow the A1062) to Bewilderwood. Bikes can be transported on the service to Hoveton station, so you can enjoy the leisurely 10-minute cycle to the site. The road is busy but a path alongside keeps you away from the traffic.

Camp at Clippesby Hall

Clippesby Hall is only a few miles down the road. It is a campsite that has a strong reputation for its commitment to the environment with a David Bellamy award for conservation. The onsite pub and shop serve local and fairtrade produce and customers can hire bicycles. The site contains some secluded spots as well as family areas and immaculate facilities. There are some wooden cabins onsite for those who prefer a roof overhead.
Address: Clippesby, Great Yarmouth, Norfolk NR29 3BL
Telephone: +44 (0) 1493 367 800
Website: www.clippesby.com

Eat at the Bure River Cottage

Between Bewilderwood and Clippesby in the quaint broadside village of Horning, the The Bure River Cottage restaurant serves locally caught fish and seafood. Try the wild Norfolk mussels in season, local grilled Dover sole or local chargrilled lobster with garlic butter.
Address: 27 Lower St, Horning, Norwich NR12 8AA
Telephone: +44 (0) 1692 631 421

Julian Claxton

The original eco boutique hotel, Strattons is a feast for the senses. The hotel treats its guests to uninhibited luxury with individual rooms that exhibit the owners' love of art and form. You'd really have to return ten times to appreciate the lavishness of each unique bedroom and suite. Period features, antiques and rich fabrics sit alongside an extensive selection of local art throughout the hotel and even in the grounds. Many of the sculptures and mosaics are made from scrap materials transformed into leaping stags or intriguing murals. This is definitely a hotel that stands out and has been admired many times over for its commitment to the environment.

The policy alone is almost tomelike and all credit goes to the staff who are more than dedicated to seeing it all through. Everything imaginable is diverted from landfill and is stored in the impressive onsite recycling outhouse ready to be distributed locally or recycled in the usual way. Organic waste ends up enriching the soil and benefiting the orchard of fruit trees including nectarine, peach, fig and grapes. The hotel also grows its own organic vegetables and herbs to supply the restaurant. Other local producers feature heavily on the breakfast and dinner menu and Vanessa encourages guests to take some produce home with them. Staff are also taken out on familiarisation trips to get to know the raw ingredients on the farms. The décor of the restaurant is inspired by the surrounding Brecks landscape which is well- suited to food and drink production.

t: +44 (0) 1760 723 845
w: www.strattonshotel.com

Julian Claxton

Contact details
Address: 4 Ash Close, Swaffham, Norfolk PE37 7NH
Telephone: +44 (0) 1760 723 845
Website: www.strattonshotel.com
Price: Singles range from £120-£130, doubles from £150-£175 and suites from £200-£225 per night. All prices include breakfast
Opening times: Year round
Disabled access: There is a ground floor bedroom with no step access

Getting there slowly
The nearest railway stations are in Norwich or King's Lynn. The First Group bus service number X1 serves both Norwich and King's Lynn stopping at Swaffham Market Place.

Visit Go Ape
In nearby Thetford Forest you could find yourself swinging from tree to tree thanks to Go Ape which offers adventures in the canopy via high wires, zip slides and rope bridges. The company ensures that the trees are well protected and visitors can learn more about the ecosystems of the forest while they're there.
Address: High Lodge Forest Visitor Centre, Near Brandon, Suffolk
Telephone: 0845 643 9215
Website: www.goape.co.uk

Beccles is an unassuming town. It's got an understated charm about it but being that bit further south is less showy than some of the more touristy villages of the Norfolk Broads. And it hides one of my favourite eco-friendly B&Bs. Just behind a row of houses on the outskirts of the town, the path opens up to a wildflower meadow on top of which floats Pinetrees. It was the vision of owners Sue and Graham, who spent years trying to find the perfect spot to build their home and welcome guests. They eventually found it in North Suffolk and worked with a local architect to ensure the build would be as environmentally friendly as possible.

The building blends perfectly into its location helped by the fact that Sue and Graham used wood from sustainable sources that will change beautifully over time. It's the sort of build Kevin McCloud would be happy to follow, charting its ups and downs to become one of the most distinctive places to stay we know about. A clever water system ensures nothing is wasted, not even rainwater, which they harvest for the toilets and cleaning. Sewage is treated onsite without chemicals and the field receives the discharged clean water.

The area around the building is positively humming with wildlife. The meadow allows nature to flourish and there's a small natural pond to attract water creatures. They have an extensive organic vegetable plot with hens to lay eggs for breakfast. The neighbours also play their part. The farmer trims the field and a Greek neighbour has supplied them with olive groves which are part of Sue and Graham's extensive tree planting and woodland management scheme. They are both keen cyclists and welcome anyone travelling the Sustrans National Cycle Network Route One.

t: +44 (0) 1502 470 796
w: www.pinetrees.net

Contact details
Address: Park Drive, Beccles,
Suffolk NR34 7DQ
Telephone: +44 (0) 1502 470 796
Website: www.pinetrees.net
Price: A double room starts at £50 per
night (single occupancy £40) and
there's a discount for cyclists, walkers
and those using public transport.
Additionally, a stay of four nights or
more earns a 10% discount but single
night stays are £5 extra
Opening times: Year round
Disabled access: On the ground floor
there is an ensuite room suitable for
disabled guests

Getting there slowly
Beccles has a railway station which is
on the Lowestoft to Ipswich line. There
are no direct trains to Norwich, but
you can catch the bus number X2 from
the main bus station in the city.

Ride a solar boat
The world's first solar-powered passenger boat named after the Egyptian sun
god Ra has been ferrying sun worship-
pers on the Norfolk Broads since 2000. She traverses the waterways of the
nature reserves silently storing power in the seven rows of panels overhead and
providing passengers with the opportunity to view the restoration taking place
on the Barton Broads, which is only possible by boat.
Address: Gay's Staithe, Neatishead, Norfolk
Telephone: +44 (0) 1603 782 281
Website: www.broads-authority.gov.uk

Eat at the Waffle House
If you spend a day in Norwich, the Waffle House is a good choice for a filling
lunch. The delectable range of sweet and savoury waffles covers all toppings
from fairtrade banoffee and hot Dutch apple to roasted red peppers and hummus and avocado. The flour used in the waffles is organically grown and
stone-ground at the local Redbournbury Mill.
Address: 39 St Giles Street, Norwich NR2 1JN
Telephone: +44 (0) 1603 612 790
Website: www.wafflehouse.co.uk

Julian Claxton

The Ecotech Centre is a hub for all things green and technological. The centre welcomes delegations of children and adults alike to get to grips with everyday sustainability. Voted as an Icon of England, the centre itself is an ecologically sound building backed by its two impressive wind turbines. The wooden structure of the Centre uses timber from sustainable sources in the UK. The Orangery is a long airy room with a mighty 1,000² m glass sloped ceiling which allows for a passive solar heating system to operate. On less sun-filled days, cascades of rainwater tumble down the window overhead and the water is collected for recycling. Along with the building's natural ventilation, nearby Thetford Forest supplies thinnings to an additional heating system. Meanwhile the northern elevation is highly insulated to prevent heat loss and the climate of the building is all cleverly controlled by a computer system.

If you've ever wondered what it's like inside a wind turbine, Swaffham-1 as it's known, is the only one in the world where you can climb to the top. The turbine stands at 67 metres in height and hides a spiral stairway up to the Norman Foster-designed public viewing platform. The panoramic views are not to be missed along with a close-up of the three tonne blades that have the capacity to provide enough electricity to power over 1,000 homes – saving over 3,161 tonnes of CO_2 per year compared to conventionally-produced power.

t: +44 (0) 1706 726 100
w: www.ecotech.org.uk

Julian Claxton

Contact details
Address: Turbine Way, Swaffham, Norfolk PE37 7HT
Telephone: +44 (0) 1760 726 100
Website: www.ecotech.org.uk
Price: Admission to the centre is free; however turbine tours cost £5 for adults and £3 for children
Opening times: Monday to Friday (excluding bank holidays) Gardens, Shop & Café Monday to Friday 10am-4pm. Turbine tours take place three times per day
Disabled access: There is disabled access throughout, except in the wind turbine

Getting there slowly
The nearest railway stations are in Norwich or King's Lynn. The First Group bus service number X1 serves both Norwich and King's Lynn stopping at Swaffham Market Place.

Eat and stay at Strattons Hotel
A short walk from the Ecotech Centre is the fine Strattons Hotel. Bold colours, fine dining, art around every corner; this is no ordinary hotel. Strattons treats its guests to uninhibited luxury with individually styled rooms. This listed villa abides by a rigorous environmental policy involving all its staff members and supporting the local community. The grounds contain an onsite recycling facility and fruit trees have been planted in every available space. The restaurant serves excellent local produce.
Address: 4 Ash Close, Swaffham, Norfolk PE37 7NH
Telephone: +44 (0) 1760 723 845
Website: www.strattonshotel.co.uk

Just down the road from Milden Hall B&B is Kentwell Hall, a place where I spent some of my dazed and confused childhood dressed up in Tudor garb and wandering the grounds of the house looking for my treble recorder. Later in life I realise that this is an accepted pastime in Suffolk and at Milden Hall you can make a holiday of it by staying in the Tudor Barn sleeping 22 people complete with cartlodge and wheeled truckle beds. The barn dates back to the 16th Century and has a roaring woodburner for chilly evenings. There's no obligation to dress up but should you wish to, the banqueting table housed in the 95ft long barn is an ideal place for a feast.

For a more conventional, but equally comfortable place to sleep, the house itself has three B&B rooms containing antique furniture and imaginative prints. In the morning you'll be greeted with a delicious home-grown farmhouse breakfast. Juliet and Christopher, as keen conservationists and (obviously) historians, have a deep respect for their surroundings and implement a host of recycling, composting and energy saving initiatives including a supply of 20 bikes to borrow. For self-caterers, they provide a family activity pack which includes outdoor activities for children such as tree hugging, pond dipping and orienteering and a bicycle treasure hunt. Adjacent to the barn is a herb garden and granary museum. Guests can also explore the orchard, ponds and meadows around the farm.

t: +44 (0) 1787 247 235
w: www.thehall-milden.co.uk

Contact details
Address: The Hall, Milden, Lavenham, Sudbury, Suffolk CO10 9NY
Telephone: +44 (0) 1787 247 235
Website: www.thehall-milden.co.uk
Price: B&B rooms start at £60 per night, barn prices on application
Opening times: Year round
Disabled access: There is no disabled access to the self-catering barns or farmhouse B&B

Getting there slowly
Sudbury railway station is about four miles from Milden Hall B&B. From there it's a 15-minute taxi journey.

Visit Hollow Trees Farm Shop
Borrow one of the 20 bikes to cycle to Hollow Trees Farm Shop in the nearby village of Semer. Here you can meet some rare breeds, walk the nature trails, buy some lovingly reared meat and visit the café and garden centre.
Address: Hollow Trees Farm Shop, Semer, Ipswich IP7 6HX
Telephone: +44 (0) 1449 741 247
Website: www.hollowtrees.co.uk

Where it all started, the Eco-lodge in Lincolnshire was where I took my first green holiday. Like myself, many guests arrive not knowing what to expect. But they leave with a clearer idea of not only the impact of travel on the environment but also their place in the environment itself. Owners, Andy and Geri, live the ethos of sustainability and have put their heart and soul into helping their guests enjoy it too at their lodge.

Andy, a seasoned woodsman built the lodge using wood from the land around his home. He continues to nurture the woodland, planting new trees and creating nature walks for his guests to learn about the wildlife. The wood also feeds the magnificent wood burning range which heats the radiators and water supply. You can leave your casserole or veggies in the oven to slow roast while you spend the day on the saddle or sitting outside on the veranda. A relaxing afternoon was spent here watching a summer storm blow over the Fens.

When the chill sets in, duck into the lodge to warm up. Once the fire gets going the lodge turns into a Scandinavian sauna. The outside privy is as luxurious as compost toilets come, stocked with recycled toilet paper, sawdust to toss down the hole and handy back issues of the Dalesman. Guests don't appear to begrudge keeping the fire going or pumping the water to fill the tank. In fact, it all adds to the adventure and brings on moments of realisation which inspire guests to think a little differently about their everyday lives.

t: +44 (0) 1205 871 396
w: www.internationalbusinessschool.net

Contact details
Address: Station Road, Old Leake,
Boston, Lincolnshire PE22 9RF
Telephone: +44 (0) 1205 871 396
Website:
www.internationalbusinessschool.net
Price: A week long stay is £340 plus
£5 per person. A long weekend is
£170 plus £5 per person
Opening times: Year round
Disabled access: There is a ramp
access at the back of the lodge, which
is all on one level

Getting there slowly
Take the train to Boston (on the Nottingham to Skegness line). From Boston
there aren't adequate public transport links to the lodge. However, Geri can
organise a pick-up from the station, or otherwise bring your bicycle and ride the
eight miles or so across the Fens.

Visit Sibsey Trader Mill
Just a couple of miles from the lodge and a landmark on the flat landscape, Sib-
sey Trader Mill makes a good afternoon out. The mill still produces organic stone
ground flour and serves the best tea in the Fens. The Mill is open April to Octo-
ber, on Tuesdays, Saturdays and Bank Holidays.
Address: Frithville Road, Sibsey, Boston, Lincolnshire PE22 0SY
Telephone: +44 (0) 1205 750 036
Website: www.english-heritage.org.uk

On the flood plain of the River Trent, one of England's most important water-ways, Attenborough Nature Centre is a haven for wildlife. Its busy network of walkways and islands criss-crosses an open expanse of water. Here sightings of usually rare Kingfishers and Bitterns are regular occurrences as are the appear-ances of otters, slowly increasing in numbers. A causeway connects the mainland with the visitor centre which opened in 2005. The award-winning building fuses design ideals of modernism such as the use of exposed angular metallic frames and glass facades with sustainable building techniques. Cleverly it compliments the wetland landscape. Photovoltaic panels on the south facing roof generate electricity and a combination of solar panels and under-water pumps produce heat. The Nature Centre houses a buzzing café serving fairtrade drinks and homemade food. There are also numerous areas for discovering more about the surrounding wildlife and sustainability. The Willows Education Penin-sula at the back of the building is rich in mini-beast wildlife and perfect for open air learning. The Centre offers regular workshops for children during school hol-idays exploring the area and wildlife.

t: +44 (0) 115 972 1777
w: www.attenboroughnaturecentre.co.uk

Contact details

Address: Barton Lane,
Attenborough, Nottingham,
Nottinghamshire NG9 6DY
Telephone: +44 (0) 115 972 1777
Website:
www.attenboroughnaturecentre.co.uk
Price: Free admission
Opening times:
Summer: Monday-Friday: 10am-5pm
Weekends: 9am-6pm
Winter: Monday-Friday 10am-4pm
Weekends: 9am-4pm
Disabled access: The centre has full
access for disabled visitors

Getting there slowly

Attenborough railway station is
within walking distance of the Centre.
From here there are direct trains to
Birmingham and Derby. From Nottingham railway station, there are
trains to Attenborough or take the
Rainbow 5 bus (direction Derby) from
the Broadmarsh Centre and get off at
Chilwell Retail Park and walk 500m
along Barton Lane.

Eat and stay at Restaurant Sat Bains

Undoubtedly the best restaurant in
Nottingham and one to blow the
budget on, Restaurant Sat Bains has a
reputation that foodies come from far
to try out. The restaurant isn't far from
Attenborough – in fact there's a scenic

river route in the summer, but whatever happens, make sure you arrive with an
appetite. After a gastronomic journey through Mr Bains' artisan courses, you can
also make use of the restaurant's chic bedrooms and stay for breakfast.
Address: Lenton Lane, Nottingham NG7 2SA
Telephone: +44 (0) 115 986 6566
Website: www.restaurantsatbains.com

The limestone village of Tideswell is an historic and often forgotten village of the Peak District. Little would you know that it could make an excellent base for exploring Britain's first National Park. An affordable and excellent eco option comes in the form of Bushey Heath Farm. A farm diversification project, Bushey Heath not only welcomes visitors to stay in the bunk barn, bothys, campsite or caravans but Rod, the owner, can show you around his impressive array of renewable energy sources and introduce you to the farm yard animals.

The first thing you'll notice on arrival is the wind turbine which produces enough power for the farm and its guests. Rod encourages recycling throughout the site, collects rainwater for WC flushing and has fitted a ground source heat pump to provide all the heating and hot water to the bunk barns. The bothys look a little like wooden sheds on stilts but offer a dry shelter when the Peak District rains close in. The bunk barns, however, provide more of a collective farm experience and with friends, this option would be good fun. The barn conversions incorporate a host of recycled building materials such as flooring, doors and stonework in the development. Camping is in the shadow of surrounding woods and there's an onsite farm shop for essential supplies.

t: +44 (0) 1298 873 007
w: www.busheyheathfarm.co.uk

Contact details

Address: Tideswell Moor, Tideswell,
Buxton, Derbyshire SK17 8JE
Telephone: +44 (0) 1298 873 007
Website: www.busheyheathfarm.co.uk
Price: The bunk barns range from
£375-£495 per week for sole use for
6-8 people. The bothys cost £25 per
night and camping starts at £4 for
adults and £2 for children
Opening times: Year round, except
campsite (Easter to October)
Disabled access: The bunk barns
aren't suitable for disabled access

Getting there slowly

Buxton railway station is a few miles
from Tideswell. Bus number 66 leaves
hourly from the station and connects
to the village. From there it's about a
mile or so walk along Manchester Road
to Bushey Heath Farm.

Visit Tindalls Bakery & Delicatessen

For a true taste of the Peak District,
this popular delicatessen in Tideswell
offers local organic meats and freshly
baked breads. The handmade pork pies
are made to a 50-year-old recipe.
Address: Commercial Road, Tideswell,
Derbyshire SK17 8NU
Telephone: +44 (0) 1298 871 351

Sally and Rob are so particular about the freshness of their eggs that they collect them fresh from two local farms, the only ones in the area to meet their exacting standards. Along with a perfect egg, the food served at this rural bed and breakfast is nothing but the real thing. The couple are adamant that food should be unadulterated and nutritious. They serve nothing processed, and encourage their guest to try unpasteurised real milk from the farm. If you mention the ordinary white stuff, be prepared to learn everything there is to know about how the milk industry makes us poorly and our cows sick. Like his insightful knowledge, Rob's menu is full of passion and more than a little influenced by his Polish roots. The breakfasts especially benefit from the Slow Food style using produce made at home by Sally and Rob or sourced within a 10-mile radius. The Cheese Flops are a house speciality.

The guesthouse itself was once a farmhouse, and the grounds contain a small, cosy self-catering cottage that used to be the cider mill. The rooms are in the process of being changed to be completely organic, so you will find hand made soaps and organic cotton sheets. Energy saving is apparent throughout and the garden is an ongoing project that attracts wildlife.

t: +44 (0) 1432 840 353
w: www.aspenhouse.net

Contact details

Address: Aspen House, Hoarwithy,
Herefordshire HR2 6QP
Telephone: +44 (0) 1432 840 353
Website: www.aspenhouse.net
Price: Double rooms start at £68 for
two nights, £64 for four nights, or
£72 for one night
Opening times: Year round
Disabled access: Ground floor
room available for those with
limited mobility

Getting there slowly

The nearest railway station is Here-
ford, just over 10 miles away which has
direct services to London. From there,
buses (the number 37) leave every
hour or so to Hoarwithy village.

Eat at New Harp Inn

As an alternative to the cosy dining
room at Aspen House, the New Harp
Inn – literally just across the road –
offers fresh food using local Herefordshire suppliers. The pub also smokes its
own produce, from rabbits to cheese, and serves an awesome range of ales
ciders and European beers.
Address: Hoarwithy, Herefordshire HR2 6QH
Telephone: +44 (0) 1432 840 900
Website: www.newharpinn.co.uk

It came as a shock to Kate Grubb when she started working for a holiday letting company and realised the amount of waste that guests left behind and their lack of interaction with local communities. Set on changing all this, she embarked on a project of her own that would see her hard work pay off in the form of a well-loved ecocabin on the family's farm. Kate's ethos is to create somewhere relaxing and cheerful to stay while drip-feeding a sizeable list of environmental and social aims that she encourages her guests to adopt. The cabin's location in the rolling hills of Shropshire immediately puts you at ease and creates a setting that makes you feel more determined than ever to protect what we've got on our doorstep.

The cabin is built with local Douglas Fir timber and homegrown Larch and insulated with British sheep's wool. Energy comes from solar panels for electricity and hot water and wood pellets for the stove. The local economy is benefiting from the 'buy local' shopping service offered by Kate along with her 'honesty' shop inside the ecocabin. And who could resist the local cider on a warm balmy evening on the veranda? The interior is fitted out with stylishly reclaimed furniture and local art and the kitchen work surface is made from recycled yoghurt pots. The environment is chemical free and the bright bedding is all the more snug for its organic cotton. There is also plenty to keep the children amused that doesn't include a TV (as there's not one provided) such as the great outdoors and an impressive selection of books and games.

t: +44 (0) 1547 530 183
w: www.ecocabin.co.uk

Contact details

Address: Obley, Bucknell,
Shropshire SY7 0BZ
Telephone: +44 (0) 1547 530 183
Website: www.ecocabin.co.uk
Price: Rates are from £420-£605 per
week or £95-£105 per night (mini-
mum two nights) for four people
Opening times: Year round
Disabled access: There are a few steps
up to the cabin, but also a ramp

Getting there slowly

There is a small train station three
miles away at Hopton Heath. Craven
Arms (nine miles) has a larger mainline
railway station. Collection can be
arranged from the railway station.

Visit the Slow Food town of Ludlow

The UK headquarters of the Slow Food
Movement is based in Ludlow, the first
town in the UK to be named a 'Cit-
taslow'. You can see why when you
visit Ludlow, as it is positively brimming with fine eateries and specialist
food shops. Throughout the year the
citizens of Ludlow organise events and
ensure that our slow food traditions in
the UK are protected.
Website: www.slowfoodludlow.org.uk

An opportunity for renovation and a passion for organics led to the rebirth of this green hotel in the heart of the Lake District. The owners of Moss Grove have taken care to restore the hotel in a sustainable way and their uncompromising level of quality and exceptional taste make this a hotel to remember.

The wallpaper throughout the hotel is not only beautiful, but is screen printed in London with natural inks. The carpets are not only soft underfoot, but are woven with Axminster wool by a firm in Kendal. And the stunning beds, almost sculptures in themselves, are made from reclaimed timbers or come from sustainable sources. Just about every feature is thought through with both the customer and the environment in mind.

The breakfast is a magnificent layout of organic cereals, seeds, breads, and a delicious mix of Mediterranean dishes including olives, feta wraps, homemade crostinis and roasted peppers. There are also local meats, cheeses and eggs and fairtrade fruit. It's an innovative and daring approach which seems to go down well with guests who enjoy the informality of the breakfast. Upstairs in the rooms, there are spa baths, natural duck down duvets and organic toiletries. The water runs like silk as it is filtered by the hotel and free of chlorine and pesticides.

t: +44 (0) 15394 35251
w: www.mossgrove.com

Contact details
Address: Grasmere,
Cumbria LA22 9SW
Telephone: +44 (0) 15394 35251
Website: www.mossgrove.com
Price: Double rooms start at £125 and
include breakfast for two people
Opening times: Year round, except
Christmas Eve and Christmas Day
Disabled access: There is no disabled
access to the rooms

Getting there slowly
There are regular trains to Windermere from Manchester and Oxenholme. Catch
the bus number 555 from the railway station and get off in Grasmere, a 20-
minute bus journey.

Eat at The Jumble Room
Grasmere has a number of eateries, but this one's a much loved choice by locals
and visitors alike. Children are most welcome here, in fact, they helped decorate
the place with their cheerful drawings. It's cosy and intimate, and the food is all
homemade and organic where possible. The fresh baked walnut and date bread
is the perfect partner to the soup of the day. The restaurant is open for lunch
and dinner.
Address: Langdale Road, Grasmere, Cumbria LA22 9SU
Telephone: +44 (0) 15394 35188
Website: www.thejumbleroom.co.uk

Once a Victorian textiles mill and now a planet friendly health spa, the Titanic in West Yorkshire offers a tempting package for wellbeing and an impressive quota of eco credentials. The wondrous array of whirlpools, steam and bubbles are powered in the greenest way possible and the treatments are all natural, if not organic. The building itself benefits from renewable natural resources like its private borehole 100 metres below the earth's surface. This deep cavity provides vast quantities of silky pure water that is filtered and pumped into the chlorine-free spa.

All the heat and the majority of the spa's electricity come from a CHP (combined heat and power) unit that takes chippings from trees managed sustainably over a controlled time period. This is the first CHP installation in a large mill conversion in the UK and extends to the contemporary residential and guest apartments above the spa where clientele can stay during their break. The rest of the electricity is powered by solar panels overhead that work throughout the year. When you're not spending much of your time drifting from one therapy to the next, the rooms offer stunning views over the Pennine Hills and the restaurant serves healthy, locally sourced meals. The organic mud chamber session comes recommended and is all about getting dirty to get clean again inspired by ancient Egyptian bathing techniques.

t: 0845 410 3333
w: www.titanicspa.co.uk

Contact details
Address: Low Westwood Lane, Linthwaite, Huddersfield,
West Yorkshire HD7 5UN
Telephone: 0845 410 3333
Website: www.titanicspa.co.uk
Price: Spa breaks start at £99 per person
Opening times: Year round
Disabled access: The founders have taken steps to ensure Titanic Spa and its
Heat Experiences are inclusive for those with disabilities, providing a hydro-
pumped chair for pool access, wide corridors, waterproof wheel chair covers
and audio loops for therapists

Getting there slowly
Huddersfield railway station is 3 miles from Titantic Spa from where there are
regular train connections to Slaithwaite railway station. From here it's a 20-
minute walk to the spa. Otherwise there are regular buses from Huddersfield
centre which stop closer to the spa.

Eat at the Mill Race
Closer to Leeds than Huddersfield, The Mill Race is holding its own with an
adventurous and enticing organic menu. Local and seasonal availability is the
driving force behind this popular eatery which draws inspiration from its York-
shire surroundings.
Address: 2/4 Commercial Road, Kirkstall, Leeds, West Yorkshire LS5 3AQ
Telephone: +44 (0) 113 275 7555
Website: www.themillrace-organic.com

NTPL/Ian Shaw

I've not been on a National Trust Working Holiday. My hectic schedule this year meant that a week's hard graft would have to wait until there was time. So instead we sent our friend Luke off to the Lake District to give it a go. Luke isn't the work shy type. He's a well experienced tree surgeon used to climbing trees in all weather conditions. So his text after the first day came as a surprise reading something like: 'hard work here, met lots of interesting people'. Oh, we thought. If Luke is being made to feel like he's working hard, then it must be a demanding holiday. All the same, he did choose dry stone walling and fence building – not the easiest of tasks. That coupled with sharing a living space with 11 other people took some guts when you're used to living on your own and working with one other person.

Fears unfounded, he came back full of stories about each of his workmates. Some he got on well with, others he found a bit overbearing at times and many with all kinds of eating habits. His tales of his companions were affectionately told which made me think that he really enjoyed the company of strangers for the week. The accommodation is basic and usually comes in the form of a bunk house with males in one room and females in the other. A cooking and cleaning rota keeps the basecamp in order and Luke gracefully embraced the task despite having barely ever cooked for more than one person before in his life. He achieved the mean feat of cooking a feast (meat and vegan) for all his housemates in one sitting. So it wasn't just the satisfaction of building miles of dry stone wall to the exacting standards of their warden, but also the camaraderie of living and getting on with others. The working holidays cover all kinds of tasks and no previous experience is necessary. You'll also get time off to explore the surroundings and the National Trust properties nearby.

t: 0844 800 3099
w: www.nationaltrust.org.uk

Contact details

Address: The Working Holidays
Booking Office, Sapphire House,
Roundtree Way, Norwich NR7 8SQ
Telephone: 0844 800 3099 (Booking
line and enquiries)
Website: www.nationaltrust.org.uk
Price: Working Holidays start at £40
for short breaks and from £80 for one
week, and include accommodation
and food but not transport
Opening times: Year round
Disabled access: It's best to check
with the individual holidays to find
out if they are suitable for disabled
travellers but generally it is necessary
to be physically able

Getting there slowly

When you book a working holiday,
you'll receive details of the nearest
railway or bus station from where you
can arrange collection to take you to
basecamp. All transport to the work
area will be arranged for you.

Unfettered access to a dressing up box and an onsite sweet shop is enough to send the most grown up of adults wild with excitement. Within minutes of arriving, one friend emerged from the marquee dressed as a walking banana and another had raided the sweety jar and was busy carrying out his transaction on the old school cash machine. I wondered where we'd arrived to find such delights at our disposal.

The answer was La Rosa: a curious wonderland of vintage caravans decked with oddments and trappings from the past. Our caravan was named Psycho Candy, and comes with paraphernalia involving Barbara Cartland and pink flamingos, not forgetting the candy pink bedding. There's a strong commitment to the environment at La Rosa. The vans are not connected to the mains, so lighting is all by candle light or by way of the special campfire. A gas cylinder for heating and cooking is all that's needed and water usage is kept to a minimum, although the showers in the old shepherd's byre are a real treat. Gypsy Martha's caravan is now the composting toilet and is a great place to fantasize about a career move to join the circus. The vans are surrounded by protected woodland and every now and then, the chugging of the North Yorkshire Moors railway can be heard in the distance. Staying at La Rosa is getting back to basics but all the same gives the imagination a good workout.

t: +44 (0) 7786 072 866
w: www.larosa.co.uk

Contact details

Address: Egton, Whitby,
North Yorkshire
Telephone: +44 (0) 7786 072 866
Website: www.larosa.co.uk
Price: £27 per person per night
Opening times: End of March until
end of September
Disabled access: Access is limited for
disabled travellers due to uneven
paths and rocky roads. There are also
steps into the caravans

Getting there slowly

The nearest mainline railway station is
Whitby although this is still eight miles
away from La Rosa. Buses run to the
nearby villages of Grosmont and Egton.
Also the North Yorkshire Moors railway
stops in Grosmont. See www.nymr.co.uk
for timetables and information. There's
also a discount at La Rosa for guests
arriving by public transport.

Drink at The Birch Hall Inn

The local pub is a real gem. It's a ten-
minute walk through the woods but
worth the journey for the friendly
Yorkshire service, pork pies and pickle,
and of course, the local ales. There's
usually a gathering of customers outside as the pub is rather on the small
side.
Address: Beck Hole, Whitby, North
Yorkshire YO22 5LE
Telephone: +44 (0) 1947 896 245

The first little pig from the Three Little Pigs story gave straw a bad name for home building. If only he knew about its super insulating properties that make it one of the best and cheapest materials around. All it needs is some lime rendering and eco-plasterboard to keep the big bad wolf out. While there are few wolves stalking the farmyards of East Yorkshire, the straw bale cabin was built to withstand the elements and offer guests a stay a little out of the ordinary. Even during the chilly nights, the cabin needs no heating as its temperature stays about 10 degrees above the outside temperature. It's something that Carol Atkinson, the cabin's owner is monitoring closely to ensure the building 'breathes' with its guests through its lime rendered walls.

Not only is straw an eco-friendly building material, but the Atkinsons have also incorporated a host of other earth-friendly features. Equipment and furnishings for the cabin are not bought new if it can be avoided. In fact, many features use bits and pieces from the farm. An old door from the barn has been transformed into beams, edging and coat hooks. The hanging rails in the wardrobe were once part of the milking parlour and the path uses a number of paving stones found on the farm. There's an inside natural toilet which uses a fan and chopped hemp to keep any odour at bay. One of my favourite features of the cabin is the honesty shop. It's basically a cupboard full of dry foods (and bottles of real ale) that are available for purchase. Arriving by train, the honesty shop is a life saver and you get to pick some free gifts up to the value of £2 each if you leave the car behind – we couldn't resist Grandma Jennie's strawberry jam and a bottle or two of cider. The Straw Bale Cabin is tasteful and well thought through from start to finish. As a guest you can't fault its eco performance, nor its comfort and attention to detail.

t: +44 (0) 1430 410 662
w: www.strawcottage.co.uk

Contact details
Address: Village Farm, Brind, Howden, Goole, East Yorkshire DN14 7LA
Telephone: +44 (0) 1430 410 662
Website: www.strawcottage.co.uk
Price: A full week stay ranges from £245 to £350. Weekends range between £150 and £165
Opening times: Year round
Disabled access: There are three steps up to the cabin as the building is literally on wheels

Getting there slowly
There are direct trains from London King's Cross on Hull Trains. Otherwise connect at Doncaster or Grantham from the north or south.

Shop at the Jug and Bottle
Using the free hire bikes at the cabin, we cycled to the nearby village of Bubwith to buy some essentials from the Jug and Bottle. In a converted village school, the Jug sells all sorts of deli-style goods including local brews on draught, local cheeses and organic vegetables.
Address: The Old School, Main Street, Bubwith, East Yorkshire YO8 6LX
Telephone: +44 (0) 1757 289 707
Website: www.jugandbottle.co.uk

NTPL/Nick Meers

Gibson Mill remained silent and still for 50 years following the Second World War until the National Trust embarked on a major restoration project reopening the Mill in 2005. From the early days of the Industrial Revolution, the mill produced cotton using Hebden Water to power its huge water wheel. As part of the restoration, the water mill is back in action and has helped this unique visitor attraction to become fully self sufficient.

The property generates its own electricity through the hydro-electric turbines and photovoltaic panels. The surrounding woodland of the Hardcastle Crags Estate, also part of the National Trust property, provides biomass fuel for heating and natural spring water trickles down the hill to provide the mill with drinking water. Even the lift is powered by the renewable energy of its human occupants through a series of pulleys and weights.

All of the grey water produced from catering and hand basins is treated by passing it through a 'soakaway'. This is a long clay pipe with holes buried about one metre underground. Wastewater seeps out of the pipe and is then naturally filtered through the soils before it can reach the local groundwater. There is also a composting toilet which uses the dry waste to fertilise the fields. Although the history of the mill remains the focus of the attraction, its green credentials offer an interesting angle to understand more about how industry and the environment interact.

t: +44 (0) 1422 844 518
w: www.nationaltrust.org.uk

Contact details

Address: Hardcastle Crags, Hebden Bridge, West Yorkshire HX7 7AP
Telephone: +44 (0) 1422 844 518
Website: www.nationaltrust.org.uk
Price: Free admission
Opening times: During school holidays Gibson Mill is open daily 11am-4.30pm otherwise weekends only. The National Trust owned estate, Hardcastle Crags, is open all year round
Disabled access: The ground floor has low, narrow doorways and uneven floors. There is a lift to upper floors

Getting there slowly

Hebden Bridge railway station has direct connections with Halifax and Manchester Victoria. Gibson Mill is a two-mile walk from the railway station.

Eat at Moyles Restaurant

In the Bo-ho town of Hebden Bridge, the restaurant at Moyles Hotel offers an inspired menu of locally sourced food under the careful supervision of head chef Daniel Derrington. The restaurant has a relaxed, but stylish atmosphere and the bar offers a tasting menu of CAMRA-approved real ales.
Address: New Road, Hebden Bridge, West Yorkshire HX7 8AD
Telephone: +44 (0) 1422 845 272
Website: www.moyles.com

NTPL/Joe Cornish

NTPL/Joe Cornish

There's nothing like bringing the beautiful outdoors inside. With panoramic glass frontages, the first group of residences by Natural Retreats does just that allowing in the greenness and light of the Swale Valley. The ten sustainably built lodges are carefully tucked into the Yorkshire Dales hillside where even the locals failed to spot them. The residences are all self-contained and the founders of Natural Retreats decided not to provide any onsite shops or bars to encourage guests to venture to the nearby Georgian market town of Richmond. Not only is the local economy benefiting, but it means that the area around the lodges is quiet and peaceful for wildlife and guests.

One of the founders is also an architect by trade which means that the lodges benefit from his sense of style and perfectionism. Upon arrival we were greeted with a sizeable hamper filled with delicious local and organic produce along with a stack of wood to get the wood burning stove going. The main living space is open plan with squeaky clean high spec furnishings. Despite the odd luxuries like TV and DVD player, the residences try hard to maintain a sense of sustainability. Full recycling facilities are provided along with natural cleaning products. Mountain bikes are also available for guests to hire for exploring the local area. Children are positively idolised at the lodges and not only have 54 acres to run around in, but also a nature trail to explore and an area where they can build dens.

t: +44 (0) 161 242 2970
w: www.naturalretreats.com

Contact details
Address: Hurgill Rd, Richmond, North Yorkshire DL10 4SG
Telephone: +44 (0) 161 242 2970
Website: www.naturalretreats.com
Price: During low season, prices start at £325 for two nights and go up to £1,100 for a week in high season.
Opening times: Year round (but note closed in 2008 until 4th July for new building work)
Disabled access: The residences only offer ground floor accommodation

Getting there slowly
The nearest railway station to Richmond is in Darlington from where there are regular buses to Richmond. From the town it's a 20-minute walk to the residences or short taxi journey.

Visit Nature's World
In nearby Middlesborough, Nature's World offers an insight into sustainable living and the future of the planet through interactive displays and themed trails. Solar-powered talking posts help visitors to navigate their way around the 25-acre site which includes a 400-metre long working model of the River Tees.
Address: Ladgate Lane, Acklam, Middlesbrough, Tees Valley TS5 7YN
Telephone: +44 (0) 1642 594 895
Website: www.naturesworld.org.uk

Eat at Seasons Restaurant
The Tudor-inspired railway station in Richmond closed to passengers in the 1960s but more recently became a new arts centre, cinema, restaurant and space for small-scale artisan food producers. Seasons Restaurant inside the old station uses local and seasonal produce with menus on a British theme.
Address: Richmond Station, Richmond, North Yorkshire DL10 4LD
Telephone: +44 (0) 1748 825 340
Website: www.restaurant-seasons.co.uk

Norwegian-inspired architecture is found at the Hytte in scenic Northumberland. Near to Hadrian's Wall, and fully accessible to disabled visitors, the Hytte ticks all the boxes for comfort, accessibility and the environment. The lodge is surprisingly spacious and cosy at the same time with its vaulted ceilings and log burning stove. It was designed to be low impact using FSC-approved timber and a turf roof for insulation and to blend in with the landscape. Along with its wood burning stove, the self-catering lodge uses a 6kw ground source heat pump and has a multi-zoned underfloor heating system. The appliances are low energy and there's a reed bed water treatment system along with extensive recycling facilities.

Meanwhile guests can make use of the sauna and hot tub from where there is ample opportunity for some star-gazing during clear nights. During the day, there's an acre of land around the Hytte to explore which is a designated wildlife area attracting populations of birds. The Hytte has everything from wider doorways and low surfaces to ensure that all disabilities are catered for.

t: +44 (0) 1434 672 321
w: www.thehytte.com

Contact details
Address: Bingfield, Hexham,
Northumberland NE46 4HR
Telephone: +44 (0) 1434 672 321
Website: www.thehytte.com
Price: For a week's stay, prices range
from £500-£850 (sleeps eight)
Opening times: Year round
Disabled access: Assessed as 'Access
Exceptional', the Hytte has achieved
the standards for both independent
and assisted wheelchair users and
fulfils additional, more demanding
requirements providing for several
levels of mobility impairment

Getting there slowly
Hexham railway station is a few miles from the Hytte. From here you can call a
bio-diesel taxi run by Eco Cabs (telephone +44 (0) 1434 600 600 or visit
www.600600.co.uk).

Visit Alnwick Garden
The Duchess of Northumberland had a vision to turn the gardens at Alnwick into
a veritable wonderland of grottos, mazes, fountains and tree houses. The result
is truly inspired. Her Grand Cascade is one of the largest water features in the
UK and water is filtered and recycled to minimise waste.
Address: Denwick Lane, Alnwick, Northumberland NE66 1YU
Telephone: +44 (0) 1665 511 350
Website: www.alnwickgarden.com

Revisiting Cumbria House in 2007, I was pleased to find that the new owners Patrick and Mavis were continuing in their predecessors footsteps by keeping Cumbria House green. This large B&B offers an affordable option for Lake District enthusiasts as there are plenty of walking and cycle routes on the doorstep. For this reason there's little need to bring the car and if you leave it behind, then expect a discount off the cost of your stay. The bus network around the Lakes links up with the railway stations of Windermere and Penrith and helps walkers to get off the beaten track. Cumbria House supports local conservation projects including the maintenance of nearby fell footpaths popular with outdoor enthusiasts. Guests at the B&B are asked to recycle their waste using the depots on each landing. There are also energy saving measures in place and the new owners have improved the building's insulation. For guests filling up on breakfast, they can be sure that the ingredients are sourced locally and there's a choice of organic and fairtrade teas. The home-baked bread rolls are delicious. They are handmade using organic, stone-ground flour from The Watermill at nearby Little Salkeld in Penrith.

t: +44 (0) 1768 773 171
w: www.cumbriahouse.co.uk

Contact details
Address: 1 Derwentwater Place, Ambleside Road,
Keswick, Cumbria CA12 4DR
Telephone: +44 (0) 1768 773 171
Website: www.cumbriahouse.co.uk
Price: £27-£33 per person per night
Opening times: Year round, except closed December-January
Disabled access: The rooms aren't suitable for disabled travellers as there's a
staircase to climb

Getting there slowly
There are bus connections with both Penrith and Windermere railway stations.
Alight in the centre of Keswick and Cumbria House is a five minute walk.

Hire a bicycle with Country Lanes
If you take the train to Windermere, Country Lanes offer cycle hire adjacent to
the railway station. There are a mix of mountain bikes and hybrids to hire – all
in excellent condition. They are available for the day or it's also possible to hire
a bike for your entire visit. The ride to Keswick is about 18 miles, but can be done
in a day.
Address: The Railway Station, Windermere, Cumbria LA23 1AH
Telephone: +44 (0) 15394 44544
Website: www.countrylaneslakedistrict.co.uk

Some would say crazy. Others suicidal. But that didn't stop me from embarking on a fully fledged outdoor adventure trip on the Pembrokeshire coast in mid-December. As a novice to any form of water activity, the thought of kayaking and coasteering (throwing oneself off cliffs into the sea) on the same day brought butterflies to my tummy. However, after a decent night's sleep at the comfortable organic eco hotel that is part of the TYF experience, I set out for a day at sea. Luckily the hotel has a shed full of the latest wetsuits and equipment which immediately put me at ease. By the time I got into the water, worries vanished and I got stuck into the adventure which had me up against numerous cliffs and jumping into swirling seas. As unnatural as it may sound, the experience was exhilarating and the thought of an organically brewed cup of tea on my return was enough to keep me in the game. A seal even popped its head above the water before I returned to harbour in my kayak.

The hotel is housed in a converted windmill and climbing to the top provides an awe-inspiring 360° view of St Davids Peninsula. TYF Eco Hotel is certified organic through the Welsh Organic Scheme. The restaurant offers locally sourced food including cheese from the next door neighbour's farm and delicious breakfasts to give you energy for the next adventure. The rooms are basic but warm and clean with a wind up radio and Ecover toiletries in the bathroom. Guests who arrive without a car can sample a free organic drink from the hotel's honesty bar. I picked an intriguing hemp beer which featured a comical scratch and sniff label. The staff wear organic cotton tee-shirts and are a friendly bunch of people.

t: +44 (0) 1437 721 678
w: www.tyf.com

Contact details
Address: TYF Eco Hotel, Caerfai Road,
St Davids, Pembrokeshire SA62 6QS
Telephone: +44 (o) 1437 721 678 (call
+44 (o) 1437 721 611 for
TYF Adventure)
Website: www.tyf.com
Price: Standard rooms cost £35 per
night and ensuite rooms start at £45.
Bar meals are available
Opening times: Year round
Disabled access: There is limited access for disabled travellers as the rooms
can only be reached by stairs

Getting there slowly
Take the train to Haverfordwest. From the railway station there are regular
buses (except on Sundays) to St Davids City. The hotel is located near to the centre of the city.

Eat at the Bench

Catering for travellers as well as locals in St Davids, the Bench has an Italian
theme inspired by owner Gianni and his wife Jo. There's a cosy atmosphere and
a varied menu including pizzas, pasta and seasonally changing homemade ice-
cream. The wine list is well-thought-through and affordable.
Address: 11 High Street, St Davids, Pembrokeshire SA62 6SB
Telephone: +44 (o) 1437 721 778
Website: www.bench-bar.co.uk

Miles of sandy beach and cliff top walks provide a playground for guests at the Druidstone Hotel and the adjoining Roundhouse. This stretch of coast is an ever changing myriad of rock pools and caves at low tide and a draw for surfers when the waves crash onto the beach. There are few views which could match the one on offer from the cliff top over St Brides Bay where you'll also find an intriguing place to spend your holidays. I couldn't decide whether guests stay at the Druidstone Hotel for the stunning scenery or the sheer entertainment value of the owners and staff with whom I spent many hours exploring the well-stocked cellars.

The owners also introduced me to their eco-cottage located further along the cliff top in a converted croquet pavilion. The Roundhouse has been standing since 1910 despite being exposed to the elements, which makes it a great place to watch storms develop over the bay particularly while dunking yourself in the wooden hot tub. The conversion was completed with a more than generous nod to the environment. The masonry heater uses wood as fuel and backs up the solar hot water system in winter. It acts as a night storage heater, slowly releasing heat over a long period of time and is more energy efficient than an open fire. The grey water toilet connects to a reedbed sewage system and lime is used instead of concrete to create a breathable structure. The timber is all harvested and seasoned from local farms and Pembrokeshire craftspeople were enlisted to help construct the stairs, fittings and doors of the Roundhouse. Natural fibre mattresses manufactured in nearby Carmarthenshire ensure a good night's sleep to the sound of waves on the beach.

t: +44 (0) 1437 781 221
w: www.druidstone.co.uk

Contact details
Address: Near Broad Haven,
Haverfordwest,
Pembrokeshire SA62 3NE
Telephone: +44 (0) 1437 781 221
Website: www.druidstone.co.uk
Price: Weekly rentals start at £315
sleeping two to four people
Opening times: Year round
Disabled access: There is an uneven
path down to the Roundhouse and a
small number of steps inside

Getting there slowly
The nearest railway station is Haverfordwest. During the summer there are regular coastal bus services calling at Druidston Haven. Or if, like me, you arrive in the depths of winter, bus services run every other day or a taxi from the railway station will cost around £17 one way.

Eat in the Druidstone Hotel
For convenience and good hearty food, the hotel has a smashing restaurant and underground bar. There are views out to sea and a menu that reflects local produce and seasonal changes. Bowls of soup and homemade bread are in high demand at lunch time and, later, you must try a locally brewed ale or two.
Address: Near Broad Haven, Haverfordwest, Pembrokeshire SA62 3NE
Telephone: +44 (0) 1437 781 221
Website: www.druidstone.co.uk

While the rest of the world has been busy depleting natural resources in the last 30 years, the Centre for Alternative Technology has been pioneering ways to build for the future. The exhibits focus on buildings, energy and organic gardening. Now building professionals and town planners alike are asking CAT for guidance on sustainable living and building. The Centre itself is buried in the trees of the south Snowdonian hills and visitors can see the work in action.

The gateway to the centre is via a steep hillside funicular that transports visitors to the summit using the power of water and gravity alone. It's the first insight we get into the Centre's mastery of engineering, exploring new ways to generate energy with those basic renewable resources: water, sunlight and wind. The exhibits focus on buildings and energy. While I explored the eco-home I overheard a snippet of conversation between child and parent, 'why don't we recycle our paper?' enquired the child. Silence, and 'well...we will do now', came the response.

So that was the power of CAT. For visitors, it's a chance to reflect, ask a few questions and come away with real ways to reduce their impact on the environment. It's not all about big builds – although the centre is undergoing its biggest project yet with the construction of a 'rammed-earth' learning and conference centre due to open in autumn 2008. It's also about the smaller ways we can save energy and be more planet friendly, such as travelling by public transport or composting our waste. Less guilt-inducing and more action inspiring, the Centre for Alternative Technology puts it all into context.

t: +44 (0) 1654 705 950
w: www.cat.org.uk

Contact details

Address: Llwyngwern Quarry,
Pantperthog, Machynlleth,
Powys SY20 9AZ
Telephone: +44 (0) 1654 705 950
Website: www.cat.org.uk
Price: Entry costs £6.40-£8.40 for
adults depending on season (conces-
sions available) and £4.20 for children
(free for children under five)
Opening times: Open all year, Easter
to October 10am-5.30pm, winter
10am till dusk. CAT closes for a winter
break in early January
Disabled access: Access to the Visitor
Centre from Easter to the end of

October is via the cliff railway which has carriages that are adapted to receive
wheelchairs. However, the path alternative is a little steep so it's best to enquire
beforehand about disabled access when the cliff railway is not operating

Getting there slowly

CAT encourages its visitors to arrive by public transport and offers a £1 discount
for those who do. The Centre is about three miles from Machynlleth train station and it's a well sign-posted and enjoyable walk. There is a bus service to the
Centre or to nearby Pantperthog from the town. Cycle hire and taxis are also
available in Machynlleth. Thanks to a partnership with ARRIVA trains, if you produce a valid train ticket from anywhere in the country to Machynlleth you will
get half price entry to the Centre.

Stay at Eco Retreats

Local tipi accommodation is provided by Eco Retreats. Expect some healing and
relaxation as part of a weekend package which includes a Reiki treatment and a
twilight meditation. You'll also receive tickets to CAT.
Address: Plas Einion, Furnace, Machynlleth, Powys SY20 8PG
Telephone: +44 (0) 1654 781 375
Website: www.ecoretreats.co.uk

Eat at the Quarry Café

As well as a wonderful café onsite, the Centre for Alternative Technology runs a
whole food café and shop in the centre of Machynlleth. The café serves a range
of organic, local, seasonal and fairtrade produce. Homemade soups are on the
menu along with light dishes and scrummy cakes.
Address: 27 Maengwyn Street, Machynlleth, Powys SY20 8EB
Telephone: +44 (0) 1654 702 624
Website: www.cat.org.uk

The mountains of Snowdonia form a natural auditorium around Bryn Elltyd guest house deep in the National Park. The house is an intriguing mix of old and new, with its wooden overhang serving as the extension. Inside the rooms use their wooden features to good effect keeping the overall feel clean and fresh. John and Ceilia are green custodians of the highest order. A solar collector hugs one outside wall of the house and provides energy to heat the water and central heating. Some trees from their own land are used in the solid fuel fire for further hot water and heating. Sewage is dealt with onsite and filters through a reed bed and into the pond. It's so clean that by the time it reaches the pond the trout live happily in the filtered water, not forgetting the toads, frogs and newts. Elsewhere in the garden, nature is allowed to flourish in all its wildness attracting insects and birds. Meat and eggs come from local farms. At the end of the garden the world famous Ffestiniog narrow gauge railway passes by every now and then and is definitely worth a go – as is the sauna at the other end of the garden.

t: +44 (0) 1766 831 356
w: www.accommodation-snowdonia.com

Contact details

Address: Tanygrisiau, Blaenau Ffestiniog, Gwynedd LL41 3TW
Telephone: +44 (0) 1766 831 356
Website: www.accommodation-snowdonia.com
Price: From £28-£33 per person per night
Opening times: Year round
Disabled access: Ground floor ensuite bedrooms are spacious with walk in
shower facilities

Getting there slowly

Bryn Elltyd is just over one mile from the mainline railway station of Blaenau
Ffestiniog. Transport can be provided from the station.

Eat at Bistro Moelwyn

The bright and cheery Bistro Moelwyn is a good option for eating out in Blaenau Ffestiniog. There are organic and local options on the menu and the
restaurant has made improvements on its environmental performance since
refurbishment installing waterless urinals, low energy light bulbs and furniture
made from sustainable rubber trees.
Address: 10 High Street, Blaenau Ffestiniog, Gwynedd LL41 3DB
Telephone: +44 (0) 1766 832 358
Website: www.bistromoelwyn.co.uk

The Apex Hotel Group has invested considerable sums of money and time into reducing the impact of their hotels on the environment. The city-based chain now has a string of awards and good practices that validate the company's claim to be green. The hotels are located in Edinburgh and London, as well as Dundee, where I was tempted by the new green spa. Although I had never thought about visiting this north easterly Scottish city, I was pleasantly surprised by the vibrancy of the place.

Not a great distance from the railway station, the Apex Hotel is a favourite for business people visiting the city. It's a dependable choice, not least for the welcoming staff and the spacious and stylish rooms. The floor to ceiling window in my room offered a great view over the regenerated harbour area and it wasn't long before I grabbed my towel to descend to the hotel's YuSpa. The Zen-like spa consists of a swimming pool, hot tubs, sauna and steam room, all of which are run on environmentally friendly principles. As expected, chemicals are kept to a minimum. The pool uses ozone as a cleaner and the hot tubs use ultra violet light. Treatment products are 100% natural and delicious-smelling toiletries are available in dispensers.

Elsewhere in the hotel, local produce is served in the restaurant and the chef tailors his menus around supplies and seasons. The hotel gives back any packaging to suppliers for reuse and ensures that they cut down on their transport miles. Apex even has its own green team led by a dedicated environmental director looking at everything from architecture and utilities, to energy consumption and supplies. New initiatives for the Apex Group will include the installation of a combined heat and power plant to save energy and of course reduce costs.

t: +44 (0) 1382 309 309
w: www.apexhotels.co.uk

Contact details
Address: 1 West Victoria Dock Road,
Dundee, Angus & Dundee DD1 3JP
Telephone: +44 (0) 1382 309 309
Website: www.apexhotels.co.uk
Price: Double rooms start at £88 per
night depending on availability
Opening times: Year round
Disabled access: There is access for
disabled visitors

Getting there slowly
Apex Hotel in Dundee is a five-minute
walk from Dundee railway station.

Eat at the Alchemy Restaurant
Housed inside the Apex Hotel, Alchemy
Restaurant offers dishes spanning the
Scottish Highlands and France. Natu-
rally, you'll find local meats and
cheeses along with an interesting
Highland tasting menu.

Address: 1 West Victoria Dock Road,
Dundee DD1 3JP
Telephone: +44 (0) 1382 202 902
Website: www.apexhotels.co.uk

Eat at Wigmores Restaurant
A little out of town, but worth the journey is Wigmores Restaurant in Broughty
Ferry. The food is unpretentious and reasonably priced, and the restaurant
makes the most of its location near to the sea serving varied seafood dishes
along with vegetarian and meat courses. There's also an extensive wine list to
compliment.
Address: 9 Erskine Lane,
Broughty Ferry, Dundee DD5 1DG
Telephone: +44 (0) 1382 774 135
Website: www.wigmoresrestaurant.com

Watching seabirds is a strangely addictive pastime; at least at the Scottish Seabird Centre it is. That's because cleverly disguised cameras have been installed on the uninhabited islands on the Firth of Foray where seabirds and animals gather in their thousands. Visitors can zoom in on the birds using the camera controls and huge screens back at the Centre. This means that the birds aren't disturbed and the voyeurs get to see a privileged close-up of wildlife in action.

The bird numbers vary throughout the year depending on the season but at certain times up to 100,000 gannets gather on the rocky islands along with colonies of puffins and seals with their newborn pups. All of the cameras on the islands are powered by solar energy and the centre itself uses wind technology to generate electricity. The regularly changing Environment Zone in the centre houses exhibits on the environment, climate change and wildlife. The puffin playzone is an area for children to explore the wildlife in a more hands-on way along with regular workshops and activities. The café has stunning views out to the Firth and its sandy beaches and serves food using local produce. The shop has recently ditched its plastic carrier bags and replaced them with jute as an example for the rest of the town's traders.

t: +44 (0) 1620 890 202
w: www.seabird.org

Contact details

Address: The Harbour, North Berwick, East Lothian EH39 4SS
Telephone: +44 (0) 1620 890 202
Website: www.seabird.org
Price: £7.95 for adults and £4.50 for children (under four free). Tickets can be booked online in advance
Opening times: Year round, except Christmas Day
Disabled access: The Seabird Centre is fully wheelchair accessible, including a lift to the Discovery Centre

Getting there slowly

Direct trains to North Berwick from Edinburgh take about 30 minutes. The Seabird Saver all-inclusive rail and day admission ticket from First ScotRail costs £8.50 for an adult and £25 for a family. For more information, visit www.firstscotrail.com. The Centre is a ten-minute walk from North Berwick railway station.

Stay at Ashdene House

A gold award winner in the Green Tourism Business Scheme, Ashdene House is an affordable B&B option just outside Edinburgh city centre. The breakfast menu consists of local meats and my favourite, the vegetarian haggis.
Address: 23 Fountainhall Road, Edinburgh EH9 2LN
Telephone: +44 (0) 131 667 6026
Website: www.ashdenehouse.com

Hotel chains aren't known for their environmental performance. However, Radisson Hotels are making considered efforts to incorporate green policies into their everyday operations. And when you consider the impact of thousands of lightbulbs across the hotel group, any reductions in energy consumption will be on a grand scale. The hotel in Edinburgh is currently leading the way under the guidance of its full-time responsible business manager. It's no easy task, especially since the hotel is located in the heart of a UNESCO World Heritage Site on Edinburgh's famous Royal Mile. Even so, working around current legislation is proving effective as the hotel saves on its energy consumption by almost 10% each month through installation of new lightbulbs and timers.

The rooms at the Radisson SAS are modern and spacious. You'll find stocks of fairtrade tea and coffee along with organic fruit and locally sourced snacks and water. Housekeeping staff are trained in ensuring that towels are only cleaned when necessary and recycling is maintained wherever possible. Each year the staff vote for a local charity to support and have a say in community initiatives. They are also offered support to use sustainable forms of transport to get to work. The hotel uses a local carbon offsetting scheme to support renewable energy projects in Scotland, paid for by Radisson SAS on behalf of conference delegates using the hotel. There's still a long way to go for the hotel, which accepts that the responsible business programme is an ongoing effort. The Rezidor Group, the owner of the chain, is now investing in sustainable design and construction for each of their new builds across the UK and abroad.

t: +44 (0) 131 557 9797
w: www.edinburgh.radissonsas.com

Contact details
Address: 80 High Street, The Royal Mile, Edinburgh EH1 1TH
Telephone: +44 (0) 131 557 9797
Website: www.edinburgh.radissonsas.com
Price: Average nightly rates come in at about £100 per room but are £220 in high season
Opening times: Year round
Disabled access: Some rooms are equipped with facilities for disabled travellers

Getting there slowly
The Radisson is centrally located in Edinburgh, just a five to ten minute walk from Edinburgh Waverley station.

Visit Our Dynamic Earth
This attraction tells an interactive story of the planet – past and present. Visitors travel through space and time to get to grips with the wonders and challenges facing the Earth today and how decisions are made that affect its future.
Address: 112 Holyrood Road, Edinburgh, Midlothian EH8 8AS
Telephone: +44 (0) 131 550 7800
Website: www.dynamicearth.co.uk

Eat at the Iglu
Food at the Iglu is at the same time wild, organic and Scottish. Charlie Cornelius, the restaurant's owner is passionate about nutritious and ecologically sound food. I opted for a bean over boar burger, although I'm told the boars were all happy ones on the farm in Glen Affric. In fact the boars are helping with a reforestation project blissfully rooting up the bracken, treading in the pine cones and fertilising the ground.
Address: 2b Jamaica Street, Edinburgh EH3 6HH
Telephone: +44 (0) 131 476 5333
Website: www.theiglu.com

The Cross is a restaurant with rooms – in that order. Clearly it's more about eating than sleeping, although sleeping soon follows an encounter with the menu downstairs accompanied by a dram or two of whisky. Located in the small Highland town of Kingussie, David and Katie are intuitive and friendly hosts. They always seem to be one step ahead of you, offering treats like a wee shortbread or a glass of fine wine. And when your defences are down, you really can't say no! David puts together a new menu every day and offers a small selection of simple dishes along with more adventurous meat and fish plates. Much of the produce is organic and traceable from the fields and waters in and around the Scottish Highlands. The wine list is a self-professed labour of love, full of carefully selected bottles including a number of organic and bio-dynamic varieties. The delicious breakfasts include freshly squeezed juice, baked croissants and hot dishes such as kedgeree, local estate venison sausages, or local black pudding with Scottish 'pancetta' and organic highland eggs.

The building itself is a former tweed mill and the owners have allowed the grounds next to the river turn into wild areas to encourage local wildlife such as roe deer, squirrels, hedgehogs, frogs, butterflies, and a large range of bird species. The rooms cut down on their energy and water usage and the bathrooms are stocked with natural toiletries. The décor is clean and basic with local art adorning the walls. Guests can enjoy their after dinner coffee and homemade petit fours in the comfortable lounge which includes stacks of games and books. Outside there's a place to play pétanque or otherwise explore the many walking trails of the Cairngorm National Park.

t: +44 (0) 1540 661 166
w: www.thecross.co.uk

Contact details

Address: Tweed Mill Brae, Ardbroilach Road, Inverness-Shire PH21 1LB
Telephone: +44 (0) 1540 661 166
Website: www.thecross.co.uk
Price: Dinner, bed and breakfast from £100 per person per night or £85 pppn for stays of three nights or more
Opening times: Closed January and Sundays and Mondays
Disabled access: There is no disabled access to the rooms, but the restaurant is on the ground floor

Getting there slowly

The Cross is a ten-minute walk from Kingussie railway station. Sleeper trains to and from London call at Kingussie on the way to Inverness. There are also regular connections to Perth. For more information, see www.firstscotrail.com.

Go skiing in the Cairngorms

Just down the road at Aviemore, Cairngorm Mountain offers some of the best skiing and winter sports adventures in Scotland. The company also operates strict environmental criteria to ensure that this beautiful mountain area is protected.
Address: Cairn Gorm Ski Area, Aviemore, Inverness-Shire PH22 1RB
Telephone: +44 (0) 1479 861 261
Website: www.cairngormmountain.org.uk

'Inspired thinking' is the philosophy behind Cove Park. In a remote location like this with views out to Loch Long, dark starry nights and all-important silence, inspiration comes easily. Cove Park was set up as an artists residency organisation but welcomes people looking for any of the above hard-to-find qualities. We arrived on foot having tried out various forms of transportation from Glasgow all of which worked seamlessly. Gradually embodiments of civilisation left us at different stages of the journey. Arriving in Cove Park, we found what we were looking for: nothing; except uninterrupted views and somewhere peaceful to stay. We found our Cube and settled in quickly.

The Cubes are a series of six converted shipping containers which provide accommodation for up to twelve guests. They are light and airy with port-holes and wide French doors which overlook a manmade lake. From the vantage point of the balcony the lake almost works as a natural infinity pool out to Loch Long. The only swimmers though are ducks who pop by for bread every now and then. The neighbouring accommodation along the hill is a pair of lodges or Pods. These sustainably built Pods were shipped directly from the set of the BBC's Castaway series in 2000 and like the cubes, have turfed roofs to create insulation and a haven for wildlife. They were also built with sustainable green oak using traditional building methods.

Cows and sheep wander around the Cubes, Pods and communal centre followed in close pursuit by Alan Lemay, Cove Park's long-serving Estate Manager. If you can get by his thick Scottish accent, Alan is a font of local knowledge pointing out nearby walks and his herd of Angus cattle. We followed his advice and covered almost the entire peninsula in the three days we spent at Cove Park, crossing its back bone and viewing Gare Loch on the other side of the hill.

t: + 44 (0)1436 850 123
w: www.covepark.org

Contact details
Address: Peaton Hill, Cove,
Argyll & Bute G84 OPE
Telephone: + 44 (0)1436 850 123
Website: www.covepark.org
Price: From £40 per night for a cube
(minimum two nights) and £120 per
night for a pod
Opening times: The residency
programme runs from May to
November each year but the
accommodation is available outside
of these months
Disabled access: There are steps and
hills to the accommodation

Getting there slowly
The journey from Glasgow takes you by bus to the small port of Gourock. Regular ferries escort passengers across the Firth and land at Kilcreggan. From there buses towards Coulport can drop you at the foot of the hill where it is just a short climb to Cove Park. Otherwise take the overnight train to Garelochead from London Euston. From the station it's a five-mile taxi journey.

Eat at the Terrace Café
One of the first sites as you arrive into Kilcreggan by ferry is the Terrace Café. And it's a good one if you're hungry. All day Scottish breakfast is served in the café featuring smoked bacon, square sausage and black pudding. They also cater for vegetarians and have a friendly quota of staff.
Address: Princes Terrace, Shore Road, Kilcreggan, Argyll & Bute G84 0JJ
Telephone: + 44 (0)1436 842 022
Website: www.terrace-coffeehouse.co.uk

Despite its remoteness in north east Scotland, visitors from around the world flock to the Findhorn Foundation to find out more about the community. And some even stay to set up home in the unique ecovillage which forms the centrepiece of the Park. The founders of Findhorn arrived in 1962 and since then the community has grown to welcome residents and visitors looking for spiritual guidance and educational programmes covering all sorts of issues from eco living to community building. It also welcomes travellers looking for somewhere peaceful to spend their holidays. The caravan park has been expanded into the ecovillage which is made up of an irregular mix of beautifully designed eco-homes some of which double up as B&Bs. The park also contains a performance venue, arts and pottery centre, and visitors can take part in the regular guided tours beginning at the Visitors' Centre. However, the best way to gain a working insight into life in the community is to participate in one of the Experience Weeks.

The Holiday Park offers caravan accommodation as well as two well appointed eco-chalets overlooking the mud flats and wildlife of Findhorn Bay. The Scandinavian-inspired chalets are on two levels with the living space at the top for optimum viewing. They are powered by the park's very own wind farm and sewage is dealt with by the awe-inspiring Living Machine. From the outside this looks like a big greenhouse, but in actual fact the plants and trees that thrive on the inside are performing the important job of treating the sewerage in the most ecologically friendly way possible. Feeling brave, I ventured inside to peer into the big barrels of sludge, plant life and varying degrees of bacterial growth. Strangely enough, it wasn't an unpleasant experience and nature's way of dealing with sewage seemed far better than a stinking sewerage plant in town.

t: +44 (0) 1309 690 311
w: www.findhorn.org

Contact details
Address: The Park, Findhorn, Moray IV36 3TZ
Telephone: +44 (0) 1309 690 311 for general enquiries or +44 (0) 1309 690 203 for the Holiday Park
Website: www.findhorn.org or www.findhornbayholidaypark.com
Price: Hire of the eco-chalets starts at £95 per night (minimum three nights) or £495 per week. Caravans start at £225 per week

Opening times: The Foundation is open all year round and the Holiday Park is open from December to October. The community store and organic café are open daily
Disabled access: Some of the paths around the park are uneven but there is access for disabled travellers in many of the buildings. The eco-chalets do not have disabled access

Getting there slowly
The holiday park is 4 miles from Forres railway station where taxis are available. Local buses from Forres also stop at the holiday park entrance.

Visit the WDCS Wildlife Centre at Spey Bay
Just along the coast at the mouth of the river Spey, dolphins and seals inhabit the waters of the Moray Firth. The beach next to the WDCS (Whale and Dolphin Conservation Society) Wildlife Centre is an excellent place to spot the wildlife and learn more about the sea creatures before slurping a mug of tea and finishing off with a colossal slice of cake.
Address: Spey Bay, Moray IV32 7PJ
Telephone: +44 (0) 1343 820 339
Website: www.wdcs.org/wildlifecentre

The only way to reach Corrour and Loch Ossian Youth Hostel is by train. In fact, the railway station is the only indication of civilisation in this remote corner of the Highlands. Descending onto the platform of the station is a bit of a heady step into the unknown but from then on the surroundings make up some of Scotland's most dramatic scenery over moors, lochs, glens and mountains. The Corrour Estate has been instrumental in keeping the rail link going since Victorian hunting days and continues to ensure that the fragile environment is protected from development and especially roads. This ethos extends to the youth hostel which opened next to Loch Ossian over 70 years ago. In 2003 the hostel was renovated to incorporate a plethora of earth friendly features and has become known as one of the greenest hostels in the country.

All the electricity for the hostel is generated by a single standing wind turbine and a multi-fuel stove provides heat and hot water. A grey water system processes water from wash-hand basins and sinks through a sand and gravel filtration system ending up in a natural reed bed. All the food waste is trapped by a sieve and transferred to one of the two on-site compost bins, to be used later as mulch for the new trees planted in the surrounding area. The dry toilet system requires no flushing and produces composted material from disposed waste. Any liquid is then evaporated using a photovoltaic solar-powered fan. The hostel itself blends in with its stunning backdrop and provides basic but comfortable accommodation for guests and walkers.

t: 0870 155 3255
w: www.syha.org.uk

Contact details
Address: Corrour, Fort William, Perthshire PH30 4AA
Telephone: 0870 155 3255
Website: www.syha.org.uk
Price: Beds cost £14 per night or the entire hostel can be rented for up to 20 people for £235 per night
Opening times: March 14th-October 12th 2008
Disabled access: There is no disabled access

Getting there slowly
Corrour railway station is on the Glasgow to Fort William line. The overnight Highland sleeper train also stops in Corrour on request. From the railway station, the hostel is located about one mile away only accessible by foot. For more information, visit www.firstscotrail.co.uk.

Eat at Corrour Station House
If eating is your first priority after jumping off the train then try Corrour Station House. Full Scottish Breakfast is served in the morning followed by hearty Highland lunches of local venison and beef. The evening à la carte menu needs to be booked in advance but offers a Scottish tasting opportunity including Clootie Dumpling and Crannachan – a creamy whisky-infused dessert.
Address: Corrour Station House, Corrour Estate, Fort William, Inverness-shire PH30 4AA
Telephone: +44 (0) 1397 732 236
Website: www.corrourstationhouse.co.uk

Off-grid and slightly off-the-wall, earthships originate in the USA and the first one to 'land' in the UK is here in Fife. Earthships are designed to generate their own natural resources like energy and food. Since they also look as if they could survive a nuclear fall-out there is a certain amount of future-proofing going on here – not that I'm suggesting nuclear war is imminent; just that we ought to think more about being self-sufficient as natural resources dwindle. Back to Earthships then and what's unique about them is that they can be adapted to almost any climate using different recycled and reclaimed materials for construction. This particular Earthship is built into the landscape to reduce its visual impact and retain heat within the building. Its walls are made from recycled earth-rammed tyres and aluminium cans. It provides its own heating, electricity, water and sewage treatment using the power of the sun, rain, and wind. The sewage is dealt with onsite by a self-contained sewage treatment system where nothing escapes into the outside environment.

The Earthship accepts visitors to wander around the building and learn about its sustainable features. Many visitors are so struck by the idea, they start scheming their own version of an Earthship. It could be the answer to low-cost housing the government has been looking for. A guided tour lasts for about an hour and there's also plenty of additional information about sustainable building in the Earthship's extensive library. Visitors can also take part in regular creative waste workshops, turning household waste into crafts, toys and arty objects.

t: +44 (0) 1592 891 884
w: www.sci-scotland.org.uk

Contact details
Address: Kinghorn Loch,
Kinghorn, Fife KY3 9YG
Telephone: +44 (0) 1592 891 884
Website: www.sci-scotland.org.uk
Price: Free admission; tours cost
£5 for adults, £3 children and
concessions
Opening times: Open every weekend
from 10am until 4pm; call in advance
or check website for weekday times
Disabled access: The Earthship is fully
accessible to disabled visitors
although disabled visitors are advised
to arrive by car

Getting there slowly
Kinghorn railway station has direct links with Edinburgh (about 40 minutes
away). From the station the visitor centre is a 15 minute walk. Note that the railway station has a footbridge and it is therefore not wheelchair or pram
accessible unless it can be carried.

Visit Craigencalt Ecology Centre
The Earthship is located on the site of the Craigencalt Ecology Centre, an interactive environmental education centre. Here children can go pond dipping and
explore the natural environment surrounding the centre. There are also some
spectacular views out to the Firth of Forth over the harbour at Kinghorn and out
to Bass Rock in the distance.
Address: Craigencalt, Kinghorn, Fife KY3 9YG
Telephone: +44 (0) 1592 891 567
Website: www.theecologycentre.org

The ecoescape slow travel toolkit

The view from the handlebars in Lincolnshire

ecoescape is all about travelling slowly

When we discover new ecoescapes, we like to travel slowly. We try to avoid airports and motorways and have spent days, perhaps weeks travelling by trains and buses. This has brought its own adventures. Like when we've missed a connection, for example, the added time in a place is more time to get to know it. When we've been on the train we've chatted to people or simply admired the view from the window.

So in this section of the guide, we've put together a useful toolkit to help you to find slow ways to travel around the UK, many of which we've tried out ourselves. There are also ideas for places to stay and visit that all try in many ways to reduce their impact on the environment.

So what is Slow all about?

The Slow Food Movement began in 1989 and is now filtering into many aspects of our modern lifestyles. Carlo Petrini established the world famous Slow Food Movement in defiance of mass-produced fast food which was having an increasingly damaging impact on health and the environment. The Movement is about exploring regional flavours and well-loved ingredients as well as spending mealtimes sharing food with other people in our lives.

Like the Slow Food Movement, slow travel celebrates regional diversity but in the context of journeys and holidays. Rather than arriving at our destinations as quickly as possible, slow travellers use the journey as an opportunity to get to know the places and people they meet along the way. So this means that sharing journeys is as important to slow travel as mealtimes are for slow food. This can only be achieved by taking the train or bus or other form of public transport. Like slow food, slow travel has less impact on the environment. It involves forms of transport like cycling and walking that have low or no carbon emissions.

Slow food at the Goods Shed, Canterbury in Kent
©britainonview/Daniel Bosworth

ECOESCAPE ACROSS THE UK

PUBLIC TRANSPORT

Transport Direct
W: *www.transportdirect.info*

Sometimes my destination seems remote so I wonder how I'm going to arrive by public transport. Where I always start when planning a trip is Transport Direct. The government-supported website incorporates every form of transport available and will map out your route from door to door. The bit which is really useful is planning the onward journey from a railway station as quite often bus timetables can be confusing. Transport Direct, however, picks out the appropriate operator and service to help you along the way.

Train Taxi
W: *www.traintaxi.co.uk*

Sometimes there really is no way of reaching a destination purely by public transport particularly if there's a five-mile walk at the other end. So it's useful to find out if a taxi can give you a lift from the station. Train Taxi has details of taxi companies serving every railway station in Great Britain including telephone numbers.

Traveline
T: *0871 2002233*
W: *www.traveline.org.uk*

If you need public transport information while you're out and about, Traveline offers a useful telephone service as well as regional websites. The call centre staff will look up your journey and give you times and routes.

National Rail
W: *www.nationalrail.co.uk*

National Rail's website can help you plan your journey by train although you can't book tickets online. There are also some offers linked to visitor attractions and hotels. You can also get up to date information about trains using Train Tracker by calling 0871 200 49 50.

The Trainline
W: *www.thetrainline.com*

Train tickets can be booked online using the Trainline's website or else by visiting the websites of any of the train operators (see www.atoc.org for a full list and links).

Plus Bus
W: *www.plusbus.info*

Plus Bus tickets can be purchased from railway stations and include the price of unlimited bus travel in the town or city to which you are travelling. They include discount prices and save the hassle of buying bus tickets when you arrive.

National Express
W: *www.nationalexpress.com*

Travelling by coach is the most environmentally friendly form of public transport in terms of carbon dioxide emissions. The National Express is the UK's main coach operator and serves hundreds of towns and cities across the country. Tickets can be purchased online and advance purchase Funfares start at just £1.

Mega Bus
W: *www.megabus.com*

Mega Bus offers mega cheap coach fares across the UK. Bookings are made online and start at £1.50 each way. The earlier you book, the more likely you are to bag a bargain. Be warned though that if you miss your bus, you can't get on another one. You'll have to buy a new ticket.

Cycling by the Waterside in Bristol
© britainonview/Pawel Libera

CYCLING

Sustrans & Cycling

W: *www.sustrans.org*

The most liberating holidays I've ever experienced involve taking my bicycle on the train and cycling where the mood takes me. This means that I'm not relying solely on public transport to get around. The feeling of having the freedom to explore places that might only be accessible by car offers an escape that puts you in touch with nature and the outdoors. Forget carbon emissions and post-holiday diets and instead enjoy lunch stops at pubs knowing that the exercise and fresh air is doing you nothing but good.

Part of the fun of a cycling holiday is roughly planning where you're going. If you need to catch the train with a bicycle, it's a good idea to find out the train operator's policy of allowing bikes on trains before you leave. Usually reservations are free of charge but there are also limits on how many cycles can be conveyed in one journey. The operator's website is a good place to find out, or visit A to B Magazine which gives a candid round-up of the bike-train policies across the country (www.atob.org.uk/Bike_Rail.html).

Depending on the length of your holiday, try to be flexible with route planning. Sometimes too much planning can leave you stuck if you take the wrong turning or discover an alternative route while you're out. The Sustrans website lists all the national cycle network routes that criss-cross the country. So you could combine a stretch of one of their suggested routes with one of your own. You can also buy books and maps from the Sustrans shop online to find out more about the best routes to take.

Finally, look out for accommodation that offers facilities for cyclists. If they display the logo below, this means that accommodation providers should have facilities like a drying room, a safe place to leave cycles and a friendly attitude toward no-carbon-travellers.

CTC – the UK's National Cyclists' Organisation

Cotterell House, 69 Meadrow, Godalming, Surrey GU7 3HS

T: *0870 873 0060*

W: *www.ctc.org.uk; www.cyclingholidays.org*

CTC is the UK's largest group of people on bikes with over 70,000 members. I'm told they come in all shapes and sizes and ages. The CTC's aim is get as many people on their bicycles as possible and to make cycling safer and enjoyable. The CTC has helped to shape transport policy through their many campaigns and they also offer cycle training and advice. CTC Cycling Holidays organise cycling trips around the UK and abroad throughout the year.

SUSTAINABLE CAR USE

Biodiesel Filling Stations

T: +44 (0) 1453 872 000

W: *www.biodieselfillingstations.co.uk*

A web site providing a list of places in the UK where people can fill their diesel vehicle with biodiesel fuel. It will list only fuel outlets which supply biodiesel which can go directly into diesel engines without engine modification. The main environmental advantage is that biodiesel is carbon neutral, so using 100% biodiesel in your vehicle means you are not adding to the global warming crisis.

Freewheelers

W: *www.freewheelers.co.uk*

A bit like a transport dating agency, Freewheelers matches passengers with drivers going the same way in the UK and in Europe. It's all done online and includes links to events taking place throughout the year where attendees can search for a lift to get there. Car sharing is a resource-efficient way to travel and can also save you money.

Streetcar

*Park House, 8 Lombard Road, Wimbledon,
London SW19 3TZ*

T: *0845 644 8475*

W: *www.streetcar.co.uk*

For urbanites who like to get away at the weekend but not needing a full-time car, Streetcar is a handy scheme which offers self-service cars for rent by the hour, day, week or month. They are reserved online or by phone, and can be collected and returned 24/7 using high-tech smartcards and a PIN.

WhizzGo Limited

*Floor 2, Cathedral Chambers, Great St George
Street, Leeds, Yorkshire LS2 8BD*

T: *0870 44 66 000*

W: *www.WhizzGo.co.uk*

WhizzGo provides a workable alternative to car ownership that is both socially and environmentally advantageous. They offer Pay-By-The-Hour cars with tax, insurance, fuel, maintenance and RAC cover included, plus exemption from congestion charges. There are WhizzGo cars situated in easily accessible locations in an expanding number of UK cities; including Leeds, York, Sheffield, London, Liverpool, Manchester, Birmingham, Worcester, Brighton & Hove and Southampton.

www.isanyonegoingto.com

Leigh, Lancashire WN7 2RE

W: *www.isanyonegoingto.com*

www.isanyonegoingto.com is a car share web site that puts travellers in touch with one another before they make a journey. Their aim is to reduce the number of cars on the roads. Their website puts members of the online community from the same geographical locations, travelling to the same destinations together.

WORKING HOLIDAYS

The National Trust Working Holidays

*Sapphire House, Roundtree Way, Norwich,
Norfolk NR7 8SQ*

T: *0870 429 2429*

W: *www.nationaltrust.org.uk/volunteering*

Build bat boxes in Shropshire, clean candlesticks at Clumber Park, build a yurt campsite in Cornwall, uncover a lost pool in Staffordshire. These are the kind of activities that National Trust Working Holidays volunteers have been enjoying for over 40 years to help maintain over 100 Trust properties and conserve the surrounding landscape for both wildlife and visitors. Not only does the environment benefit, but the opportunity to learn new skills and meet new friends has sustained a healthy stream of participants over this time. For more insight into working holidays and ecoscape ⬛ see pages 88-89.

Waterway Recovery Group (WRG)

*PO Box 114, Rickmansworth,
Hertfordshire WD3 1ZY*

T: *+44 (0) 1923 711 114*

W: *www.wrg.org.uk*

Advertised as a 'dirty weekend', canal camping with the Waterway Recovery Group involves restoring derelict inland waterways of Britain and of course, meeting new people and learning new skills along the way. Volunteers can learn anything from laying bricks and driving dumper trucks to learning how to manage the vegetation through scrub-bashing. All their hard work pays off when people can enjoy the canals once again.

Worldwide Opportunities on Organic Farms (WWOOF)

PO Box 2675, Lewes, East Sussex BN7 1RB

T: *+44 (0) 1273 476 286*

W: *www.wwoof.org.uk*

The UK branch of WWOOF offers UK residents and non-residents the chance to get their hands dirty and work on an organic farm. You'll be fed and watered in return for your hard labour which could involve anything from digging up vegetables and hedgelaying to building and bread-making. Be prepared to work hard and learn some new skills while enjoying being out in the natural environment.

SUSTAINABLE TOURISM

English Heritage

PO Box 569, Swindon, Wiltshire SN2 2YP

T: *0870 333 1181*

W: *www.english-heritage.org.uk*

Stewards of the built environment, English Heritage have an important remit to ensure historic sites are maintained and preserved. This includes a number of green spaces ranging from town gardens and public parks to the great country estates. English Heritage also helps the aged among trees ensuring that veteran trees and hedgerows are protected and remain a valuable part of the English landscape.

The RSPB Centre at Rainham Marshes, Essex
© Howard Vaughan

Forestry Commission

Head Office, 231 Corstorphine Road,
Edinburgh, Lothian EH12 7AT

T: *+44 (0) 131 334 0303*
W: *www.forestry.gov.uk*

Whether you believe that Robin Hood is a fictional character or real life hero, the forests of Britain are an important environment for wildlife as well as humans. The government recognised the importance of the woodlands and forests and set up the Forestry Commission to help protect and expand them. Now more than ever forests feature in people's holiday plans and you'll find an abundance of campsites and holiday parks set deep in forests and glades to enjoy uninterrupted seclusion beneath the trees.

Green Tourism Business Scheme

Green Business UK Ltd, 4 Atholl Place, Perth
PH1 5ND

T: *+44 (0) 1738 632 162*
W: *www.green-business.co.uk*

A not-for-profit company established to promote green tourism and to run the Green Tourism Business Scheme. The Scheme provides businesses operating primarily in the tourism industry with awards (gold, silver or bronze) according to their commitment to the environment. The company also promotes sustainable tourism and works closely with government and non-government organisations. Look out for their award logos in this guide.

Landmark Trust, The

Shottesbrooke, Maidenhead,
Berkshire SL6 3SW

T: *+44 (0) 1628 825 920*
W: *www.landmarktrust.org.uk*

The Landmark Trust is responsible for taking old and endangered buildings into their care to preserve them. Following restoration many of the buildings are available to rent as self-catering holiday accommodation. This helps pay for the upkeep of them. Landmarks are carefully furnished to fit the surroundings and feature open fires and lots of history to get stuck into.

Tourism Concern

Stapleton House, 277-281 Holloway Road,
London N7 8HN

T: *020 7133 3330*
W: *www.tourismconcern.org.uk*

Tourism doesn't always benefit communities around the world. Sometimes our holidays can in fact accentuate poverty in certain countries. Tourism Concern helps address these issues and look for ways to make the tourism industry fairer for people living in holiday destinations. Although Tourism Concern on the whole deals with issues overseas, their campaigns can also relate to tourism structures closer to home.

The Travel Foundation

The CREATE Centre, B-Bond Warehouse,
Smeaton Road, Bristol BS1 6XN

T: *+44 (0) 117 927 3049*
W: *www.thetravelfoundation.org.uk*

The Travel Foundation works with UK travel companies in order to make tourism a force for good – minimising any negative effects on the environment and using income from tourism to help protect precious natural resources.

GREEN HOLIDAYS

Feather Down Farm Days

Various farms arcross the UK

T: *+44 (0) 1420 80804*
W: *www.featherdown.co.uk*

Feather Down Farm holidays erect luxury tents on working farms throughout the UK. They are managed by the farmers and their families who demonstrate a commitment to the environment to maintain rural areas and nature reserves. Rather than a basic camping experience, they offer some 'extras' like a wood-burning stove, coffee grinder and comfy beds with duvets. Each Feather Down Farm has an 'honesty' shop in which fresh regional produce is sold and a place where guests can gather eggs from the resident hens. They are suitable for families and sleep up to six people.

Forest Holidays

Forestry Commission, Bath Yard,
Derbyshire DE12 6BD
T: *+44 (0) 131 314 6100*
W: *www.forestholidays.co.uk*

The Forestry Commission looks after the forests of Britain. The Commission wanted to prevent widespread ecological and environmental damage and so regularised camping in several clusters throughout the forests across the UK. These clusters formed the beginnings of the Forest Holidays sites they operate today. Forest Holidays offers cabins and camping accommodation including newly installed tree houses which feature hot tubs and private verandas. There's usually a wide choice of outdoor activities to take part in including pony trekking, walking and cycling.

Youth Hostels Association (YHA)

Trevelyan House, Dimple Road,
Matlock, Derbyshire DE4 3YH
T: *+44 (0) 162 959 2600*
W: *www.yha.org.uk*

The Youth Hostels Association operates a network of more than 200 Youth Hostels across England and Wales. It's not only an economic option but also an eco-friendly one since the YHA ensures that its hostels are not resource intensive. Some of their properties feature extensive earth-friendly practices like installing solar panelling for energy and using local produce on the menus.

FOOD & DRINK

National Farmers' Retail & Markets Association (FARMA)

12 Southgate Street, Winchester,
Hampshire SO23 9EF
T: *0845 45 88 420*
W: *www.farma.org.uk; www.farmersmarkets.net;*
www.farmshopping.com

There are now far too many farmers' markets in the UK to list in ecoescape. So a great place to find out if there is a farmers' market near to your holiday destination is through FARMA – the national Farmers' Retail and Markets Association. FARMA supports and promotes the full spectrum of direct selling activities including farmers' markets, farm shops, Pick-Your-Own, home delivery and internet sales.

HELPFUL WEBSITES & BLOGS

Green Traveller

W: *www.greentraveller.co.uk*

Richard Hammond, editor of Green Traveller, is the Guardian newspaper's Ecotravel Correspondent. The Green Traveller website features many of Richard's in-depth articles on environmentally friendly and fairtrade travel. He also invites readers to take a view and contribute to the debate on travel and the environment.

LoCo2

W: *www.loco2.co.uk*

LoCo2 is a website and blog dedicated to low carbon travel and adventures throughout Europe and beyond. On the website you can buy rail passes and get the lowdown on travelling to European festivals overland or by sea.

The Slow Traveller

W: *www.lowcarbontravel.com*

Ed Gillespie took a career break in 2007 to pursue a low carbon travel epic around the globe. On his website he tells the stories of his adventures and continues to promote awareness of the benefits of slow travel.

The Man in Seat 61

W: *www.seat61.com*

Mark Smith has become known as the Man in Seat 61 since he set up a website that helped travellers go by train anywhere in the world. The website has an enormous following and gives loads of practical advice about train travel.

Inside a tent on a Feather Down Farm holiday

the South West

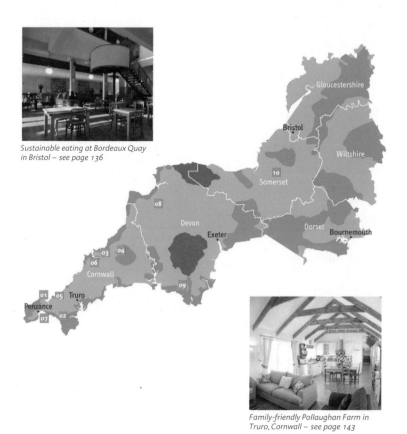

Sustainable eating at Bordeaux Quay
in Bristol – see page 136

Family-friendly Pollaughan Farm in
Truro, Cornwall – see page 143

The South West

GO SLOW
IN THE SOUTH WEST

As one of the UK's favourite holiday destinations, you would imagine that travellers are drawn to the counties of Devon, Cornwall and Somerset because of the slow pace of life and chance to enjoy some escapism. While this may indeed be the case, the clogged-up roads of the South West are not the ideal place to begin and end a holiday. While researching this book, I travelled to the South West slowly – by this I mean by public transport and bicycle. And the experience was good. Surprised? I found that the train journeys were among the most beautiful I had ever experienced and the buses travelled the country roads with views out to sea.

SLOW TRAVEL OPTIONS

Cross Country Trains – the long distance link-up
W: *www.crosscountrytrains.co.uk*
Cross Country Trains link the South West with towns and cities in the North and Midlands. So if you're travelling from Birmingham, you can settle into your seat, doze off and wake up in Exeter, or even Penzance. It's also one of the most attractive train journeys in the UK, hugging the south coast in places like Dawlish in Devon.

First Great Western – overnight and off-peak
W: *www.firstgreatwestern.co.uk*
First Great Western Trains are investing more money into the infrastructure and performance of their trains. You can also travel overnight to Penzance from London Paddington on the Night Riviera Sleeper Service.

South West Trains
W: *www.southwesttrains.co.uk*
South West Trains is playing its part in protecting the environment – and not just by providing a sustainable means of transport. The company positively encourages travel by bicycle and has increased the amount of cycle storage at its stations.

Scenic Railways of Devon and Cornwall
W: *www.carfreedaysout.com*
Scenic Railways of Devon and Cornwall is a website that brings together all of the smaller regional routes offering ideas for car free days out and linking up to walking routes. The Rail Ale Trail links these routes up to CAMRA-approved pubs making for more of a wobbly day out.

Western Greyhound Buses
T: *+44 (0) 1637 871 871*
W: *www.westerngreyhound.com*
Greyhound buses zip around the scenic roads of Cornwall linking up popular destinations like Boscastle, Bude and Newquay. Their timetables are easy to follow and buses are usually hourly which gives you plenty of time to explore the pretty towns and harbours while you wait.

Fal River Links
W: *www.falriverlinks.co.uk*
Fal River Links is a car-free co-operative in the Truro, Falmouth and Roseland area of the South West. Its aim is to get people out of their cars and reduce congestion in this area of Cornwall. Many of the local attractions like the National Maritime Museum are accessible by boat and so Fal River Links works with them to provide regular water services and promote their car free discounts to customers. The boat service links up with many walking trails, cycle routes (all the boats take bicycles) and the Cornwall Coastal footpath.

BRISTOL

Places to Eat

Bordeaux Quay
V-Shed, Canons Way, Bristol BS1 5UH
T: *+44 (0) 117 906 5550*
W: *www.bordeaux-quay.co.uk*
Bordeaux Quay is located in a converted shipping shed and is a sleek and sustainable restaurant, brasserie, deli and cookery school. Seasonality and traceability support the restaurant's dedication to reducing its food miles sourcing many of its ingredients from around the West Country. Recycling, solar panels and rainwater harvesting also help the restaurant to reduce its impact on the environment.

Boston Tea Party
75 Park Street, Bristol BS1 5PF
T: *+44 (0) 117 929 8601*
W: *www.bostonteaparty.co.uk*
West Country café chain, Boston Tea Party, has four 'cafs' including this popular outlet in Bristol. The seasonally sympathetic menu of homemade food

uses suppliers from around the West Country and imports fairly-traded tea and coffee. The garden comes alive in the summer months adding to the laid back atmosphere of the place.

Café Maitreya

89 St Mark's Road, Easton, Bristol BS5 6HY
T: *+44 (0) 117 951 0100*
W: *www.cafemaitreya.co.uk*

Love of food and a love of life at Café Maitreya helps this restaurant in Bristol to stand out in a crowd. The menu is vegetarian and follows a strong ethos of organic, seasonal and wild. There are some adventurous flavours and dishes here like the rhubarb and sweet potato gratinée or the sauté parsleyroot and Harlech cheese paupiettes. As much energy is dedicated to the wine list which features a good selection of organic varieties.

Carpe Diem Restaurant & Champagne Bar

Millennium Parade, Explorer Lane,
Bristol BS1 5TY
T: *+44 (0) 117 316 9173*
W: *www.thecarpediem.co.uk*

In the throbbing heart of Bristol, Carpe Diem provides an all-round ethical dining experience. From the food and furniture to the coffee and cutlery, every detail of the eatery has been carefully selected to ensure that its impact on the planet is as small as possible. On the menu, there are adventurous plates of local and organic produce like the Slow Roasted Saddle of Duchy Mutton and Baked Cauliflower in Cheddar Gorge Cheddar Sauce.

Prince of Wales

5 Gloucester Road, Bishopston, Bristol BS7 8AA
T: *+44 (0) 117 924 5552*
W: *www.powbristol.co.uk*

The organic menu at the Prince of Wales is testimony to JJ the landlord's dedication to keeping food free of the bad stuff. He has even branched into producing his own organic lager – Charlie's Pride. The pub operates an eco-friendly policy including biodegradable bin bags, waterless urinals and a 100% organic wine list.

CORNWALL

Places to Eat

Archie Browns

Bread Street, Penzance, Cornwall TR18 2EQ
T: *+44 (0) 1736 362 828*
W: *www.archiebrowns.co.uk*

Archie Browns, a vegan and vegetarian café, is responsible for pushing Penzance's status as a fairtrade town and is itself a beacon for 'conscious consumption'. Their local procurement policy is complimented by a string of environmental measures. For body and soul, Archie Brown's is a busy little health food shop and therapy space.

Bay Restaurant

Britons Hill, Penzance,
Cornwall TR18 3AE
T: *+44 (0) 1736 366 890*
W: *www.bay-penzance.co.uk*

Overlooking Penzance Harbour, Bay Restaurant naturally makes use of its seaside location and serves AA rosette-standard dishes specialising in seafood. The menu includes delights such as Newlyn-Landed Roast Skate Wing with Saffron, Smoked Salmon and Flageolet Bean Nage and Grilled Fillet of North Atlantic Turbot. The restaurant celebrates Cornish produce in their Local Heroes Menu.

Blas Burgerworks

The Warren, St Ives,
Cornwall TR26 2EA
T: *+44 (0) 1736 797 272*
W: *www.blasburgerworks.co.uk*

Not your usual burger joint. These tasty patties, both meaty and vegetarian, are all cooked with local ingredients. The beef is naturally reared and free range. The restaurant has a strict recycling policy and composts much of its waste. The atmosphere is relaxed and informal as diners gather round reclaimed timber tables. For vegetarians, the sunflower burger is a definite hit.

Tree camping at the Mighty Oak, Cornwall

feel good

With more 'guilt-free green' choices than any other part of England, the South West is the perfect place to have a 'feel good' holiday with a lighter footprint.

THE
Green
Tourism
BUSINESS SCHEME

For hundreds of places to stay, visit, eat & drink, look for the leaf and visit:

www.visitsouthwest.co.uk/feelgood

South West
England

Harbour Lights Fish and Chips

Arwenack Street, Falmouth, Cornwall TR11 3LH
T: +44 (0) 1326 316 934
W: www.hlfish.co.uk

Proving that takeaway food doesn't have to be harmful to the environment, Harbour Lights sources its fish from sustainable stock and has ditched its polystyrene trays in favour of card-board versions which are said to keep the batter crispier for longer. The harbour views are a real bonus to these hearty fish and chips.

The Windswept Café

South Fistral Beach, off Esplanade Road,
Pentire , Newquay, Cornwall TR7 1QA
T: +44 (0) 1637 850 793
W: www.windsweptcafe.co.uk

As the name implies, the Windswept Café enjoys its unique position overlooking the beach at Newquay. Enjoy a homecooked chunk of cake while admiring the sea views which don't get much better than this. The Café uses local seasonal produce to reduce food miles, home-bake all their dishes and recycle what little packaging is leftover.

Places to Visit

Eden Project

Bodelva, St Austell, Par, Cornwall PL24 2SG
T: +44 (0) 1726 811 911
W: www.edenproject.com

Eden Project is home to Britain's best-loved biomes. Helping to bring sustainability to the lives of many, this world-renowned attraction explores many aspects of the natural world and our place within it. Eden is truly a sensory experience that invites you to touch, taste and smell. An annual pass to the Humid Tropics Biome is a sure way to beat winter blues without ever stepping foot out of the country. Arriving by bicycle or public transport brings significant discounts with more money to spend on the vast selection of recycled goods in Eden's tempting store. Everywhere you turn, there is evidence of the attraction's aim to become waste neutral and self-sufficient; from colour coded recycling outlets, to solar photovoltaic panels and wind powered toilets.

National Maritime Museum Cornwall

Discover Quay, Falmouth, Cornwall TR11 3QY
T: +44 (0) 1326 313 388
W: www.nmmc.co.uk

The National Maritime Museum has created a unique focal point for visitors to discover the long maritime heritage enjoyed by the population of

Inside the warm temperate biome at the Eden Project, Cornwall

Cornwall. The design of the building is inspired by its subject matter through the use of sustainable ship building materials such as local slate and green oak boarding clad by master shipwrights. It has also been designed around a natural ventilation system which removes the need for air conditioning. In the winter the building's thermal mass helps maintain a highly efficient under floor heating system. Visitors can climb to the top of the look-out tower for breathtaking views over the harbour, docks and estuary and sail model boats in an all-weather simulator pool.

The Lost Gardens of Heligan

Pentewan, St Austell, Cornwall PL26 6EN
T: +44 (0) 1726 845 100
W: www.heligan.com

The gardens of the Heligan estate were in swift demise at the end of the 1980s and it was only because a collection of strange etchings were discovered in one of the walled gardens that imaginations began to go wild. Slowly the stories of those who worked and lived on the estate began to unveil themselves as the restoration of the gardens began. Today there are over 80 acres of grounds to explore including a magnificent vegetable garden and exotic glasshouses.

Activities

Cornwall Soapbox

Unit 6, Foundry Farm, Foundry lane, Hayle,
Cornwall TR27 4HD
T: +44 (0) 1736 758 358
W: www.cornwallsoapbox.co.uk

Nestled amongst 16 arts and craft workshops in Hayle, Cornwall Soapbox produces and sells organic handmade soaps and natural skincare products. Suzanne, the owner, runs workshops throughout the year from her shop so you can learn how to make your very own shampoo soap bar and return home with something 100% made in Cornwall.

Elemental Tours

11 Alverton Terrace, Penzance,
Cornwall TR18 4JH
T: *+44 (0) 1736 811 200*
W: *www.elementaltours.co.uk*

The Atlantic coast off Land's End and the Lizard Peninsula is home to diverse species of marine wildlife like sharks, whales and dolphins. To see these amazing creatures up close, tour operators need to take responsibility to ensure that minimal disturbance is caused. Elemental Tours takes visitors out on boat trips to get to know the wildlife but also ensures that does no damage in the process. They do this through raising money for local wildlife charities as well as being accredited with the Wildlife Safe Scheme award (WiSe) which demands a strict code of conduct around the animals. Elemental Tours also run low emission boats and use eco-friendly cleaning products.

Fal River Links

2 Ferry Cottages, Feock, Truro, Cornwall TR3 6QJ
T: *+44 (0) 1872 861 914*
W: *www.falriverlinks.co.uk*

Fal River Links is a car free co-operative in the Truro, Falmouth and Roseland area of the South West. Its aim is to get people out of their cars and reduce road pollution and congestion in this rather narrow area of Cornwall. The car-free network serves both local people and visitors. Many of the local attractions are accessible by boat and so Fal River Links works with them to provide regular water services and also promote their car-free discounts to customers. Using Fal River Links services you can reach the National Trust Trelissick Garden, National Maritime Museum, Trebah Garden, and Truro Cathedral and many waterside pubs and restaurants. The boat service also links up with many great walking trails, cycle routes (all the boats take bicycles) and the Cornwall Coastal footpath.

Global Boarders

Lowena, Chynoweth Lane, St Hilary, Penzance,
Cornwall TR20 9DU
T: *0845 330 9303*
W: *www.globalboarders.com*

Learn to surf with the green and family friendly Cornish surf school. All accommodation is eco-friendly and their policy is to minimise CO_2 emissions and use local suppliers. Beginners are welcome and holidays can be taken over a week or for a city getaway, a weekend break. **For more insight into ecoscape** 07 **see pages 38-39.**

Places to Stay – Hotels, Self-Catering & B&Bs

Bangors Organic B&B

Bangors House, Poundstock,
Bude, Cornwall EX23 0DP
T: *+44 (0) 1288 361 297*
W: *www.bangorsorganic.co.uk*

The first Soil Association-certified B&B and tearoom, Bangors offer organic lunches and tea along with swish rooms for staying guests. The grounds surrounding the house produce an abundance of organic vegetables and are managed in a way to encourage the wildlife. Bed linen, towels and robes are all made from organic cotton and are great way to end an evening spent in the roll-top Victorian bath.

Bedknobs

Polgwyn, Castle Street, Bodmin,
Cornwall PL31 2DX
T: *+44 (0) 1208 77553*
W: *www.bedknobs.co.uk*

On a quiet leafy road in Bodmin, Bedknobs offers elegant and spacious B&B accommodation. The rooms are furnished with antique pieces and lush quilts. In the bathroom you'll find organic and chemical-free toiletries, all of which have been part of owner Gill's long-term research project to find high standard environmentally friendly suppliers. The snug rooms are heated using an energy efficient gas boiler and solar panelling takes care of the hot water. **For more insight into ecoscape** 06 **see pages 36-37.**

Bedruthan Steps Hotel

Mawgan Porth, Cornwall TR8 4BU
T: *+44 (0) 1637 860 555*
W: *www.bedruthan.com*

With breathtaking views over the North Cornish Coast, Bedruthan Steps Hotel is situated on National Trust coastline overlooking the golden sands of award-winning Mawgan Porth beach. Bedruthan has an array of leisure facilities including indoor and solar-heated outdoor pools. Bedrooms are designed with contemporary comfort, with views over the Atlantic Ocean. The Indigo Bay Restaurant serves the best of seasonal local produce accompanied by an impressive wine list. Children can interact with the environment in the nature garden and a Real Nappy Kit is available for guest use. A wealth of staff-led recycling initiatives and low energy lighting are implemented throughout.

Bosayne Guest House

Atlantic Road, Tintagel, Cornwall PL34 0DE
T: *+44 (0) 1840 770 514*
W: *www.bosayne.co.uk*

GOLD

Just 300 metres from the north coast of Cornwall, Bosayne Guest House has eight bedrooms and a self-catering cottage. The Walker family take lots of small steps to reduce the impact of their business on the environment including energy saving initiatives and waste reduction. Bread for breakfast is all home baked topped with Cornish butter, honey from Portreath, and locally made marmalade and jams.

Boswednack Manor

Zennor, St Ives, Cornwall TR26 3DD
T: *+44 (0) 1736 794 183*
W: *www.boswednackmanor.co.uk*

Boswednack Manor looks out to a wild stretch of North Cornish coast that is lined with magnificent cliffs and coves to explore. The B&B rooms all boast privileged views out to the horizon with organic meadows and gardens in the foreground. Solar panels provide energy needed to heat the water and the hosts offer guided wildlife walks. The farmhouse also has a self-catering annex for up to five guests.

Botelet Farm

Herodsfoot, Liskeard, Cornwall PL14 4RD
T: *+44 (0) 1503 220 225*
W: *www.botelet.com*

With a wide choice of accommodation, Botelet Farm appeals to a wide audience. There are two stony cottages for traditionalists, bed and breakfast for escapists and yurts for adventurists. Mineral water is pumped from deep below the orchard and repairs are carried out using traditional and recycled materials. Timber is coppiced from the hedgerows to supply the open fires and around 1,000 trees and hedging plants are planted each year. Organic matter is thrown on the compost and fed to the vegetable garden.

View from the pool of Bedruthan Steps Hotel, Cornwall

Buttervilla

Buttervilla Farm, Polbathic, St Germans, Torpoint, Cornwall PL11 3EY
T: *+44 (0) 1503 230 315*
W: *www.buttervilla.com*

Buttervilla is an organic farm set in fifteen-acres of beautiful countryside. The owners care for their land in a sustainable, natural and eco-friendly way and have an abundance of wildlife to help you feel close to nature. They have never used chemical sprays so the environment is clean, pure and influenced by the Atlantic breezes with the south Cornish coast just two miles away. Local seasonal produce is served for breakfast and evening meals including the freshest day-caught fish, with everything sourced from organic suppliers whenever possible. Robert is also passionate about tomatoes and grows his own heritage varieties.

Castallack Farm

Lamorna, Penzance, Cornwall TR19 6NL
T: *+44 (0) 1736 731 969*
W: *www.castallackfarm.co.uk*

Castallack is a small farm located on the Land's End Peninsula. Owners, Nick and Rachel run their B&B and self-catering cottages on the farm. The couple make sure that waste is minimised through recycling and composting and the farmhouse breakfasts feature offerings from the farm or nearby village. Nick and Rachel also breed Ryeland sheep, geese and free range chickens. They even keep Chico, the Llama who helps protect the lambs from foxes.

Coriander Cottages

Old Watermill, Penventinue Lane, Fowey, Cornwall PL23 1JT
T: *+44 (0) 1726 834 998*
W: *www.coriandercottages.co.uk*

Coriander Cottages used to be part of an old watermill and cyder barns. Today they are a formidable set of self-catering properties all recently renovated to a high specification – aethestically and environmentally. They are powered by a ground source heat pump, solar panels and 100% green tarrif and have been finished with a traditional lime render and insulated with local sheep's wool. The two-acre wildlife garden surrounding the cottages is an ongoing project and will soon become a nature trail around badger setts and ponds.

East Penrest

Lezant, Launceston, Cornwall PL15 9NR
T: *+44 (0) 1579 370 186*
W: *www.organicfarmholiday.co.uk*

Children can run wild on the organic farm at East Penrest among ancient oak woodland, streams and acres of space. Accommodation is in a roomy converted barn and provides a traditional setting for a family holiday. Guests can even lend a hand on the farm and learn more about tasks such as lambing, haymaking or hedge-laying.

Goongillings Cottages

Nancenoy, Constantine, Falmouth,
Cornwall TR11 5RP

T: +44 (0) 1326 340 630

W: www.goongillings.co.uk

Goongillings is an organic farm with a collection of traditional self-catering cottages as well as a restored gypsy caravan. The farm contains over 150-acres much of which is woodland brimming with wildlife to explore including populations of badgers, foxes, buzzards and waterfowl. It is also has its own private quay on the River Helford. The cottages are kitted out with wood stoves and antique furniture. The 'Showman's Caravan' is a romantic alternative on wheels.

Higher Lank Farm

St Breward, Bodmin, Cornwall PL30 4NB

T: +44 (0) 1208 850 716

W: www.higherlankfarm.co.uk

Supporters and wearers of Real Nappies, the Finnemore children have played a crucial role in the 'greening' of Higher Lank farm. The real nappy service is offered along side other child friendly fittings and feeding times. The farm offers hands on experience for children as they get to know a variety of animals, all accustomed recipients of children's attention. The Nursery Rhyme self-catering cottages were completed in 2005 adhering to green criteria throughout with high-specification insulation above your head and under floor heating below your feet. Wood burning stoves offer deliciously slow cooked meals using the farm's own wood supply.

Lantallack Farm

Landrake, Nr Saltash, Cornwall PL12 5AE

T: +44 (0) 1752 851 281

W: www.lantallack.co.uk

If you like art then you'll love Lantallack Farm. Nicky is the lady with the paintbrush and she's happy to assist her B&B guests to get creative during their stay. The Cornish view consisting of meadows, wild flowers, valleys and streams has more than enough inspiration for artists to get stuck into. Otherwise the farmhouse and its solar heated swimming pool provide alternative places to relax. Nicky and Andrew serve breakfasts using eggs from the hens, bread straight from the Aga and local organic meat.

Little Callestock Farm

Zelah, Truro, Cornwall TR4 9HB

T: +44 (0) 1872 540 445

W: www.callestockcourtyard.com

The self-catering barns at Callestock Farm have been converted with bags of character and taste. Liz and Nick, owners of the organic dairy farm run their business in a secluded rural area and have retained some of the traditional character of the barns with original pine beams, exposed stonework and wooden floors. The couple can provide organic produce including farmhouse butter, cornish preserves, cornish water and fresh organic farm eggs. There are gardens for the children and whirlpool baths for the adults.

Making Waves

3 Richmond Place, St Ives, Cornwall TR26 1JN

T: +44 (0) 1736 793 895

W: www.making-waves.co.uk

Making Waves is a bright and cheerful self-catering appartment close to the harbour at St Ives. When Simon, the owner, ran a guesthouse from here, he built a reputation for serving up the best vegan breakfast in St Ives. As it turned out, I was one of the last guests to sample his vegan bangers and I'm certain they'll be missed by his regular guests. In 2008, however, Simon is concentrating on welcoming guests to his self-catering appartment and perhaps he'll pass on a tip or two about vegan sausages that hold together in the pan. **For more insight into ecoescape 05 see pages 34-35.**

Old Solomon's Farm

Latchley, Gunnislake, Cornwall PL18 9AX

T: +44 (0) 1822 833 242

W: www.oldsolomonsfarm.co.uk

The Apple Loft on Old Soloman's Farm provides the base for a B&B stay in the stunning Tamar Valley. Host Mike is known as the Cornish breakfast king as well as being a font of all local knowledge. He serves up farm-produced eggs and bacon along with tales of the local mining history. The organic farm is teaming with wildlife, has solar panels for electricity and a bore hole for all their grey water needs.

Orchard Lodge

Gunpool Lane, Boscastle, Cornwall PL35 0AT

T: +44 (0) 1840 250 418

W: www.orchardlodgeboscastle.co.uk

Newcomers to the B&B trade, Shelley and Geoff, owners of Orchard Lodge B&B began their new life in Cornwall in 2006. **GOLD** They chose Boscastle which has a steady influx of visitors to the harbour area of the town.

Orchard Lodge is perched on top of the hill and offers modern and fresh accommodation. Shelley and Geoff have a long list of local suppliers and cook up delicious local breakfasts for guests. **For more insight into ecoescape** 03 **see pages 30-31.**

Pollaughan Farm

Portscatho, Truro, Cornwall TR2 5EH
T: *+44 (0) 1872 580 150*
W: *www.pollaughan.co.uk*

GOLD

Pollaughan Farm self-catering cottages have been lovingly restored with both children and the environment in mind. The relaxed working farm provides its guests with round the clock interaction with nature and wildlife; from fetching the eggs for breakfast to putting the donkeys to bed at night. The cottages facilitate energy saving practices at every opportunity and prove that luxury is still top of the agenda in the spacious and accessible buildings. An Aga-prepared meal using ingredients from the surrounding area and meat from the farm is one of the temptations offered by Pollaughan's hosts.

Inside one of Pollaughan Farm Cottages, Cornwall

Primrose Valley Hotel

Porthminster Beach, St Ives, Cornwall TR26 2ED
T: *+44 (0) 1736 794 939*
W: *www.primroseonline.co.uk*

GOLD

A stone's throw from the beach, Primrose Valley Hotel embodies the nouveau chic of St Ives. Tastefully decorated individual rooms and harbour views make for a memorable break by the sea. All the fish comes from sustainable stocks and the hotel makes regular donations to the Marine Conservation Society. They are also supporters of the Cornwall Wildlife Trust and raise funds by donating all the profits from the sales of environmentally friendly Jute beach bags. **For more insight into ecoescape** 01 **see pages 26-27.**

Rezare Farmhouse

Rezare, Launceston, Cornwall PL15 9NX
T: *+44 (0) 1579 371 214*
W: *www.rezarefarmhouse.co.uk*

SILVER

Rezare Farmhouse has a licence to thrill with its list of carefully selected wines, ales and ciders from local producers in Cornwall. Located in the Tamar Valley – an area of outstanding natural beauty – the owners of the B&B firmly believe in 'fostering a sense of place' by supporting local communities, minimising energy consumption, and minimising waste. Evening meals are available most nights and use locally sourced produce, some grown in the back garden. A visitor payback scheme allows customers to donate to the Tamar Grow Local scheme and apple juice has recently replaced orange juice as a more sustainable choice for breakfast refreshment.

The Hen House

Tregarne, Manaccan, Helston,
Cornwall TR12 6EW
T: *+44 (0) 1326 280 236*
W: *www.thehenhouse-cornwall.co.uk*

GOLD

A farmhouse B&B and self-catering barn in the Lizard Peninsula, the Hen House enjoys a secluded spot for guests to enjoy some traditional Cornish hospitality. Hosts Sandy and Gary souce food locally and even teach Tai-Chi to guests in the setting of their pretty wildflower meadow. They also offer holistic therapies during the quieter months. The couple help teach sustainable tourism at the local college and are both active members of the Helston community.

The Olive Tree B&B

Maders, Callington, Cornwall PL17 7LL
T: *+44 (0) 1579 384 392*
W: *www.theolivetreebandb.co.uk*

The friendly owners of the Olive Tree, Tim and Elaine, like nothing better than to ensure their guests de-stress and relax while in their care. Elaine offers complimentary therapies and an optional massage on arrival. Tim is the farmer and tends to the resident sheep and chickens, which provide fresh eggs for breakfast served on the veranda overlooking the garden. Tim and Elaine encourage use of public transport and will help guests to plan a day out by bus or train.

Trelowarren

Mawgan, Helston, Cornwall TR12 6AF
T: *+44 (0) 1326 222 105*
W: *www.trelowarren.com*

Trelowarren is believed to be one of the world's first environmentally friendly timeshare and self-catering estates offering sustained occupancy throughout the year along with commendable environmental standards. The estate aims to be carbon neutral thanks to the installation of the impressive seven-tonne biomass boiler which provides all the necessary heating for the entire 38-property site using wood coppiced from the estate's own woodland. Rainwater is harvested for eco dishwaters and washing machines and ultra efficient wood burning stoves are installed in all of the properties. **For more insight into ecoescape 02 see pages 28-29.**

Wooda Farm

Crackington Haven, Cornwall EX23 0LF
T: *+44 (0) 1840 230 140*
W: *www.woodafarm.co.uk*

Wooda Farm is the type of place where you can relax and enjoy some seclusion. It's also the kind of place you start to think differently about things and even hatch a new life plan. Owners of Wooda Farm, Max and Gary, are well aware of the conditions needed for people to feel inspired and creative. So as well as running their organic farm, they have converted a farmhouse for accommodation and have built a unique wooden studio on stilts away from distractions of modern life. Their barn also transforms into a micro-venue for performances or the odd party. The farm serves its own home-reared and grown produce, generates electricity through a wind turbine and uses water from their own spring.

The Stable Studio at Wooda Farm, Cornwall

Wringworthy Cottages

Morval, Looe, Cornwall PL13 1PR
T: *+44 (0) 1503 240 685*
W: *www.wringworthy.co.uk*

The original barns of Wringworthy Farm were converted into self-catering cottages and are surrounded with green, green grass – a perfect setting for children to run wild. The conversions were carried out sympathetically to the buildings and surroundings and contain original beams and stonework. The cottages are set around a swimming pool heated by solar panelling. The Spencer family ensure the impact of the cottages is minimised through extensive recycling and energy saving practices.

Places to Stay – Campsites & Holiday Parks

Cornish Tipi Holidays

Tregeare, Pendoggett, St Kew,
Cornwall PL30 3LW
T: *+44 (0) 1208 880 781*
W: *www.cornishtipiholidays.co.uk*

Perfect your pow-wow routine at the site of Cornish Tipi Holidays where you can enjoy the luxury of a tipi in your own private clearing. The surprisingly spacious tipis complete with Turkish rugs and lanterns offer all you need for comfort under canvas. The wood for the structures is sourced locally and hot water for the showers is powered by solar and wind technologies. The setting is car-free and buzzing with life. Take a swim or row a boat in the man made lake, once part of the quarry which has now become the site for the 37 tipis.

Cutkive Wood Holiday Lodges

St. Ives, Liskeard, Cornwall PL14 3ND
T: *+44 (0) 1579 362 216*
W: *www.cutkivewood.co.uk*

Guests staying in one of the six cedar-clad holiday lodges at Cutkive Wood have over 41 acres of Cornish countryside and woodland to play with. Owners Andy and Jackie have spent many years looking after their patch of Cornwall by enhancing the diversity of fauna and flora on their land for their guests to enjoy. The well-equipped lodges have views out to the fields and are surrounded by mature gardens.

Lower Treave

Crows-An-Wra, Penzance, Cornwall TR19 6HZ
T: *+44 (0) 1736 810 559*
W: *www.lowertreave.co.uk*

Lower Treave is a friendly, family-run campsite on

The lodge and surroundings at Cutkive Farm, Cornwall

the western extremes of Cornwall. Two miles from the beach on the Land's End Peninsula, the site has been awarded the prestigious David Bellamy Award for conservation. The Bliss family have made sure that native species of trees have been allowed to flourish and established 'wildlife corridors' by planting hedgerows seperating pitches. They also encourage recycling and waste reduction.

Out in the Open

Lower Dacum Farm, Porkellis, Helston, Cornwall TR13 0PD

T: +44 (0) 1326 340 627
W: *www.outintheopen.co.uk*

Out in the Open in every sense, this campsite has all the eco-credentials and a gay-friendly setting. Everyone's welcome here but the site is never overcrowded as owners Dee and Cath ensure that it stays as relaxed as possible. Since 1999 they have implemented a strong recycling policy and come up with ways to compost waste and reduce water consumption. Tipis and tents are available to hire and there's plenty of opportunities to explore the countryside as the campsite is situated at the start of the Lizard Peninsula.

Plan-It Earth Holidays

Chy ena, Sancreed, Penzance, Cornwall TR20 8QS

T: +44 (0) 1736 810 660
W: *www.plan-itearth.org.uk*

A Mongolian yurt camp in West Cornwall is a good place to introduce the family to some fun eco-living. Plan-It Earth have two yurts for hire with generous discounts for guests arriving by public

transport. Each yurt has its own separate kitchen tent and open fire. There are compost toilets for campers along with showers heated by wood-burning fire.

South Penquite

Blisland, Bodmin, Cornwall PL30 4LH

T: +44 (0) 1208 850 491
W: *www.southpenquite.co.uk*

South Penquite is a 200-acre organic working hill farm situated high on Bodmin Moor. The family-run farm offers a site for camping and a set of Mongolian yurts for hire. The eco-friendly shower block delivers solar heated rainwater into cubicles lined with sheets of recycled plastic bottles and yoghurt pots. Aside from this there are basic facilities and fantastic views over Bodmin Moor. The four locally built yurts are named after the three bears (Baby, Mummy, Daddy and Goldilocks) and sleep between two and six people.

The Mighty Oak

The Gardens, Nanswhyden, St Columb Major, Cornwall TR8 4HT

T: +44 (0) 1637 880 466
W: *www.mighty-oak.co.uk*

Climb to your bed at the Mighty Oak Tree Climbing Company. Here guests can fall asleep to the sound of the wind in the trees and wake up to a personal serenade of bird call. Alan Stock, a trained arborist and his wife Bethany will teach you the ropes before leading you safely to your 'tree boat' suspended 35 feet up in a tree overlooking the Cornish landscape. Experience a rare, yet exhilarating feeling of isolation which requires nothing but your own will and energy source to get you to bed.

Cornish Yurt Holidays

Greyhayes, St Breward, Bodmin, Cornwall PL30 4LP

T: +44 (0) 1208 850670
W: *www.yurtworks.co.uk*

A side step off the shaded Camel Trail cycle route, Cornish Yurt Holidays is tucked away on the edge of Bodmin Moor. Two richly decorated sleeping yurts and an opulent, yet simple bathroom yurt offer an experience under canvas that brings you closer to nature without compromising comfort or the environment. Leave the electricity supply behind and enjoy meals by candlelight and the warmth of the wood burner. **For more insight into ecoescape 04 see pages 32-33.**

The restaurant at Riverford Field Kitchen, Devon

DEVON

Places to Eat

Riverford Field Kitchen

Wash Barn, Buckfastleigh, Devon TQ11 0LD
T: *+44 (0) 1803 762 074*
W: *www.riverford.co.uk*
Riverford Field Kitchen connects the field with your plate as you eat surrounded by the latest seasonal offerings. Lunch or supper is accompanied by a tour of the farm which celebrates biodiversity and seasonally changing landscapes. Bookings are essential.

Venus Beach Cafés

Head Office: Unit A Block B, Halwell Business Park, Halwell, Totnes, Devon TQ9 7LQ
T: *+44 (0) 1803 712 648*
W: *www.venuscompany.co.uk*

GOLD
Sustainable eateries on the beach are provided by the Venus Company. Operating in Devon and Cornwall, there are Venus outlets on the beaches of East Portlemouth, Bigbury on Sea, Tolcarne and Blackpool Sands. They all serve fresh local food and work by a rigorous environmental policy including reducing packaging and recycling waste. They serve cooked breakfasts along with organic burgers and traditional pasties and pies.

Yarde Café

East Yarde, Near Torrington, Devon
On the Tarka Trail in Devon you'll stumble upon the Yarde Café at East Yarde. It's an organic eatery famous for keeping walkers and cyclists on the trail fed and watered. The little café has a composting toilet and reed bed system as part of its efforts to maintain its small section of the Tarka countryside. David, the owner has also recently opened an eco-friendly bunkhouse next to the café.

Activities

Canoe Adventures

Harberton, Totnes, Devon
T: *+44 (0) 1803 865 301*
W: *www.canoeadventures.co.uk*

GOLD
South Devon has miles of tidal rivers and creeks. That's why local Phil Sheardon decided to set up a canoe company to take visitors out on the rivers to paddle along some of the most scenic areas of Devon. The canoes take to the water quietly which means that participants have the opportunity to spot plenty of wildlife. Phil ensures that the wildlife isn't disturbed and the rivers he uses are protected.

Tarka Trail

Devon
T: *+44 (0) 870 608 5531*
W: *www.tarka-country.co.uk*
Devon's answer to Bambi, Tarka the Otter is the hero of the long acclaimed children's book by Henry Williamson. Although over 80 years old, the story of Tarka the Otter continues to inspire walkers and cyclists to explore the unchanged landscapes of North Devon. The Trail is over 180 miles in length following part of the Devon Coast-to-Coast route. Since the trail has been part of a long-term sustainable tourism project, it has benefited from ongoing management to allow the wildlife on the embankments and verges to flourish. **For more insight into ecoscape 08 see pages 40-41.**

Places to Stay – Hotels, Self-Catering & B&Bs

Ashridge Farm Holidays

Ashridge Farm, Sandford, Crediton, Devon EX17 4EN
T: *+44 (0) 1363 774 292*
W: *www.ashridgefarm.co.uk*

SILVER
Modern accommodation with a traditional farming twist, Ashridge Farm is a fully working organic farm of 190-acres. Hosts Jill and Richard have converted the farmhouse B&B using eco-friendly materials including sheep's wool for insulation, natural water based paint and wood treated with natural oils and resins. All heating, including the under floor and hot water is provided by a wood pellet burning

system. Jill and Richard protect and enhance the wildlife on the farm through a government funded stewardship scheme.

Beeson Farm Holiday Cottages

Kingsbridge, Devon TQ7 2HW

T: +44 (0) 1548 581 270

W: www.beesonhols.co.uk

Green living meets rustic charm at Beeson Farm holiday cottages. Self-catering accommodation is in converted barns and a Georgian stone farmhouse. By using traditional building products and techniques in the renovation of the buildings, much of the historical appeal has been retained including exposed stonework, natural slate shelves and lime plaster. The Farm has surrounded itself with its own wildlife nature reserve using traditional earth-friendly farming methods.

Cuddyford

Rew Road, Broadpark, Ashburton, Devon TQ13 7EN

T: +44 (0) 1364 653 325

Cuddyford is a family-run vegetarian bed and breakfast in Dartmoor National Park. Adam and Suzie cook good wholesome food including home-baked bread, free range eggs, honey from their own hives and organically grown fruit and vegetables.

Highdown Organic Farm

Highdown Farm, Bradninch, Exeter, Devon EX5 4LJ

T: +44 (0) 1392 881 028

W: www.highdownfarm.co.uk

Highdown is an organic farm with two self-catering cottages and a cosy barn hideaway. The latter is a former cider press and perfect for a couple looking for seclusion. Guests can watch the dairy cows being milked and sample some of the white stuff at breakfast. There's also an abundance of wildlife on the farm and guests can make use of a local organic delivery service.

Higher Wiscombe

Southleigh, Colyton, Devon EX24 6JF

T: +44 (0) 1404 871 360

W: www.higherwiscombe.com

The restored stone barns at Higher Wiscombe make a stylish choice for self-catering accommodation in Devon. Located in a stunning area of outstanding natural beauty, the trio of barns were once part of an apple winery. The restoration of the cottages

used local flint and timber, recycled bricks and oak from the original barns. Fallen trees on the 52-acre estate feed the wood burning stoves while a 500-year old oak tree has been designated one of the Great Trees of East Devon. The recycling facilities and buy local food schemes help guests to reduce waste and support the local community. The estate's springs feed a non-chemical bio plant providing clean water for the cottages.

Hill Cottage

Beer Mill Farm, Clawton, Devon EX22 6PF

T: +44 (0) 1409 253 093

W: www.selfcateringcottagesdevon.co.uk

The Greens at Hill Cottage live up to their name by ensuring that their self-catering cottages and new eco-barn have as little impact on the environment as possible. Elaine and Dick started out in 2000 by growing organic vegetables, looking after the wildlife and setting up nature trails. 2008 sees the opening of their converted barn which features extensive insulation, ground source heat pump, rainwater harvesting system and solar panels. The barn sleeps up to ten people and is kitted out with organic bedding and beautifully reclaimed furniture.

Hillhead Farm

Ugborough, Ivybridge, Devon PL21 0HQ

T: +44 (0) 1752 892 674

W: www.hillhead-farm.co.uk

Hillhead Farm is home to a farmhouse bed and breakfast in the South Devon countryside. The farm supplies the B&B with home produce including eggs and vegetables, so breakfast is fresh and local. The living room features a wood burner and views out to the hills. David and Jane waste practically nothing as all leftovers end up feeding the animals.

Little Comfort Farm

Braunton, Devon EX33 2NJ

T: +44 (0) 1271 812 414

W: www.littlecomfortfarm.co.uk

Jackie and Roger have created a corner of tranquility on their North Devon organic farm. The farm animals are a real draw for adults and children alike who can feed them and collect eggs for breakfast. Home grown and reared produce from the farm is available for guests in the self-catering cottages. Each of the five cottages features wood fires and private gardens. The farm generates some of its own energy through a wind turbine and looks after the wildlife inhabiting the grounds and buildings.

Norwegian Wood Organic Bed & Breakfast

Berry Pomeroy, Totnes, Devon TQ9 6LE

T: *+44 (0) 1803 867 462*

W: *www.organicbedandbreakfast.info*

Norwegian Wood is an organic B&B with views over Dartmoor National Park. Host Heather Nicholson is a nutritional therapist which means that all dietary requirements are catered for – vegan, lacto, vegeterian and wheat-free included. Heather cooks up traditional English breakfast using organic produce and uses natural cleaning products throughout the house.

Places to Stay – Campsites & Holiday Parks

Churchwood Valley Holiday Cabins

Wembury Bay, Plymouth, Devon PL9 0DZ

T: *+44 (0) 1752 862 382*

W: *www.churchwoodvalley.com*

GOLD

The wooden holiday cabins at Churchwood Valley harmoniously blend in with the landscape at Wembury Bay having been built with wood from their own abundant supply of elms, pines and chestnuts. The Monterey Pine is a familiar sight on the Devon coast and here it is used for fencing throughout the holiday village. The compost generated from day-to-day activity gives vitality to the flowers and shrubbery which are fed using conserved rainwater. **For more insight into ecoescape** see pages 42-43.

DORSET

Places to Stay – Hotels, Self-Catering & B&Bs

Cowden House

Frys Lane, Godmanstone, Dorchester, Dorset DT2 7AG

T: *+44 (0) 1300 341 377*

W: *www.cowdenhouse.co.uk*

Surrounded by organic farms in rural Dorset, Cowden House B&B benefits from a constant supply of organic produce. Breakfasts therefore are a delight and fully vegetarian. Up to six guests can be accommodated here and there's use of the pretty gardens surrounding the house. Otherwise picturesque villages aren't far away and the coast is just a 30-minute journey.

GLOUCESTERSHIRE

Places to Visit

Daylesford Organic Farmshop

Daylesford, Near Kingham, Gloucestershire GL56 0YG

T: *+44 (0) 1608 731 700*

W: *www.daylesfordorganic.com*

The farmshop at Daylesford provides a day out in itself. There's an abundance of organic produce on sale including cheese from the creamery, freshly-picked vegetables and fruits in season. The restaurant on the farm serves all this up in healthy dishes and sandwiches and in the summer the food can be enjoyed al fresco in the sunny courtyard.

The Organic Farm Shop

Abbey Home Farm, Burford Road, Cirencester, Gloucestershire GL7 5HF

T: *+44 (0) 1285 640 441*

W: *www.theorganicfarmshop.co.uk*

A complete organic experience. Start with a visit to the farm shop and café, selling the farm's own seasonal vegetables, meat, eggs, home cooked cakes and cut flowers. Continue with a nature trail walk or stay in the farm's cottage or yurt in a woodland clearing. The Farm Shop building is also available to hire and features a solar and wood chip heating system, soya based paints and low energy lighting.

SOMERSET

Places to Eat

Demuths Vegetarian Restaurant

2 North Parade Passage, Bath, Somerset BA1 1NX

T: *+44 (0) 1225 446 059*

W: *www.demuths.co.uk*

The vegetarian menu at Demuths transports customers around the world from their plate. Choices include Greek spanakopita parcels, Vietnamese risotto and an Ethiopian platter made up of pancake-style bread, dhal and spicy vegetables. Ingredients are fairtrade, local where possible and organic. The owners also run a vegetarian cookery school so you can pick up some of their tips and tricks.

The water mill at Gant's Mill, Somerset

Truffles Restaurant
95 The High Street, Bruton, Somerset BA10 0AR
T: *+44 (0) 1749 812 255*
W: *www.trufflesbruton.co.uk*

The friendly young husband and wife team that run Truffles restaurant are adamant that local food is the back bone of their business and is what keeps the food fresh and tasty. The menu at Truffles is entirely dependant on what the locals can supply and don't be surprised to see customers pop by with a bag of damsons, or whatever else they've harvested that day. The restaurant is also handily located along the fish run to Bath and Bristol from the south coast and so has a regular supply of seafood and fish. The only ingredient sourced from outside the West Country is duck which travels from Suffolk.

Places to Visit

Mill on the Brue
Trendle Farm, Bruton, Somerset BA10 0BA
T: *+44 (0) 1749 812 307*
W: *www.millonthebrue.co.uk*

SILVER

Mill on the Brue is a place for children to let go and get some fresh air. There are outdoor activities on offer like canoeing in the river and zip slides as well as opportunities to do some gardening and help with digging up some organic vegetables. Children can camp in the grounds and make use of the solar-powered drying room. **For more insight into ecoescape 10 see pages 44-45.**

Places to Stay – Hotels, Self-Catering & B&Bs

Bloomfield House
146 Bloomfield Road, Bath, Somerset BA2 2AS
T: *+44 (0) 1225 420 105*
W: *www.ecobloomfield.com*

This grand Georgian house in Bath has been converted into a sustainably managed hotel and conference centre. Hosts, Karen and Robert co-founded Bath's Farmers Market and went on to open Bloomfield House. Here they ensure all the food served is organic, local and fairtrade where possible. The hotel car runs on used vegetable oil and the garden furniture is made of sustainably-grown wood. Guests who travel to the hotel by long distance public transport or bicycle are offered a 10% discount off the standard bed and breakfast rate.

Gant's Mill
Bruton, Somerset BA10 0DB
T: *+44 (0) 1749 812 393*
W: *www.gantsmill.co.uk*

The wheels at Gant's Mill have provided power to century's of wool, silk and corn production. Its present sixth generation miller diversified into electricity production and now the mill has become both a small scale hydropower scheme and the site of a bed and breakfast and self-catering property. The 65-acre farm invites its guests to participate in its seasonal activity such as lambing in spring or haymaking in June. The mill and eccentric colour themed gardens are also open to visitors during the summer months where the gentle flow of water is apparent throughout.

Nut Tree Farm
Stoughton Cross, Wedmore,
Somerset BS28 4QP
T: *+44 (0) 1934 712 404*
W: *www.melvynfirmager.co.uk*

The 16th Century farmhouse B&B on Nut Tree Farm is set in two acres of semi-wild gardens and orchards. There's plenty of space to find some peace and quiet or engage in artistic endeavours inspired by the farm's resident woodturner, Melvyn Firmager. Natural products are used throughout and the farm also has a secluded self-catering cottage.

Lower Shaw Farm
Old Shaw Lane, Shaw, Swindon,
Wiltshire SN5 5PJ
T: *+44 (0) 1793 771 080*
W: *www.lowershawfarm.co.uk*

Lower Shaw Farm offers vegetarian weekend breaks and activity holidays for individuals, groups, and families. Actvities include everything from yoga and massage to song-writing and juggling. There are vegetable, herb, and flower gardens to relax in and basic accommodation comes in the form of chalets, caravans, and farmhouse rooms.

THE NEW FOREST
relax • explore • enjoy

rush hour

Every route in the New Forest is the scenic route.
From winding wooded lanes to the big sky of our
open grazing land, even Monday's look bright.

It doesn't get greener than this.

visit our website for a free guide
thenewforest.co.uk/eco

the South East & London

Exotic plants at the Living Rainforest, Berkshire – see page 153

Waterhouse Restaurant – a central London green eatry – see page 161

The South East & London

Be Inspired by the South East

With one third of the south east of England designated as National Parks or Areas of Outstanding Natural Beauty, it is no wonder that green and sustainable tourism features so highly in the region's many destinations and attractions. There are hundreds of ways to enjoy environmentally responsible breaks in the beautiful countryside and coastal areas that are unique to the region:

Get out of the car
Walking, cycling and riding are great ways to see the area without adding to traffic. Consider using public transport if you can, and try exploring what's on the doorstep of your destination.

Get a flavour of the area
Why not enjoy local food, drink and other products of the area while you're here?

Relax and switch off
Help us reduce light pollution, energy use and CO_2 emissions by switching off lights and standby buttons when you don't need them. Help us reduce water consumption by using just the water you need. And then relax and enjoy your break …

Look out for the Leaf
The Green Tourism Business Scheme (GTBS) encourages tourism businesses to care for the local area and environment, rigorously assessing them and giving a Gold, Silver or Bronze Award, depending on the level of good practice they achieve. By using GTBS accredited businesses you will also be making a contribution to keeping the South East special.

You won't be disappointed!

For further information visit www.visitsoutheastengland.com and click 'green'

South East | ENGLAND

GO SLOW IN THE SOUTH EAST & LONDON

More so than anywhere else in the UK, there tends to be two waves of travellers on public transport around the South East: those who travel for work and those who travel for leisure. This means that you have to choose your timings carefully to bag some cheap tickets and quieter services on public transport. For London, in particular, travelling by public transport is usually the norm for holiday travellers as driving can be a daunting experience for the uninitiated.

SLOW TRAVEL OPTIONS

Transport for London
W: *www.tfl.gov.uk*
The first place to go for information about getting around London by tube, rail, bus or boat is Transport for London. If you can log on to the internet, it's fairly easy to plan a journey by any of the means above or else check for journey updates. As the 2012 Olympic Games approach, we await better transport links than ever to bring the UK's capital up to 21st Century standards. Travelling along the Thames on the Hop-on, Hop-off services is a great way to bag great views of London between Westminster in the West and Greenwich in the East.

Pedicabs in London
W: *www.londonpedicabs.com; www.chariotbikes.org*
Sometimes short journeys between restaurant and theatre are best taken by pedicab. These are human powered rickshaw-style taxis that generally can be hailed down in London's West End and Soho. It's a fun way to see the capital by day or night and the pedicabs usually zip around rather than getting caught up in traffic.

The Big Lemon – Brighton
W: *www.thebiglemon.com*
An eco-friendly take on the yellow bus, the Big Lemon is a new service that links Brighton with Falmer and Old Steine in East Sussex. The buses are the brainchild of local entrepreneur Tom Druitt who is running the vehicles using locally sourced cooking oil as fuel. Tom is expanding the network to cover further destinations in East Sussex.

Breeze up to the Downs
W: *www.buses.co.uk*
On Sundays and Bank Holidays, Brighton and Hove Bus Company operate a service to various beauty spots on the South Downs. These include Devil's Dyke, Stanmer Park and Ditchling Beacon. The journey takes about 30 minutes and buses leave every hour.

Slow travel to the New Forest
W: *www.thegreenforest.co.uk; www.thenewforest.co.uk*
Not only does the New Forest have national park status, but the local tourism board is encouraging visitors to arrive by public transport. Railway stations in places like Brockenhurst and Beaulieu have the advantage that they are already in the sticks so you can walk or cycle directly from the platform. There are numerous places to hire bicycles (try Country Lanes on pages 62 – 63) and discounts are available at various B&Bs and hotels for travellers arriving by public transport.

BERKSHIRE

Places to Visit

The Living Rainforest
Hampstead Norreys, Berkshire RG18 0TN
T: *+44 (0) 1635 202 444*
W: *www.livingrainforest.org*
The Living Rainforest brings a taste of the tropical to Berkshire to help visitors understand how these crucial ecosystems work and why our behaviour affects their survival. You can see Britain's largest frog enclosure or be amazed at the giant water 'platter' lily which stretches a whopping eight feet across. This fascinating portrayal of life beneath the undergrowth celebrates the labours of the Leafcutter ants and the 'narcotic' effects of giant millipedes. The attraction also reveals the true cost of logging and the implications of coffee, banana and cocoa production. The Living Rainforest charity has been a fierce supporter of sustainable development since its opening having spent years understanding how to cultivate the tropical plants without pesticides and to provide shelter for endangered species, some of which have been rescued by HM Customs.

The South Downs

This iconic and internationally important landscape ranges from ancient woodland, heaths and open grassland to the dramatic cliffs at Beachy Head. A short train journey from London and Brighton, the South Downs has great bus and rail links to help you explore the area once you're here. There are wonderful trails to walk or cycle and many other outdoor activities to enjoy including horse riding, hot-air ballooning and paragliding.

www.southdownsonline.org

The Kent Downs Area of Outstanding Natural Beauty

Stretching from the London and Surrey borders through the county of Kent to the iconic White Cliffs at Dover, the Kent Downs is a special landscape with inspirational, far reaching views. This is an area of ancient woodlands, secluded dry valleys, farmed landscapes and chalk pasture, scattered oasts and orchards.

Easy to reach by train, why not discover the Kent Downs on foot and follow one of our many walking routes. Tread the paths of pilgrims along the North Downs Way, or breathe in the sea air along the Saxon Shore Way. Stay in green graded accommodation, sample the wonderful range of fresh local produce and explore our wealth of heritage. Opportunities abound for horse riding, cycling and even gliding.

www.kentdowns.org.uk

KENT
DOWNS

Area of
Outstanding
Natural Beauty

NATURAL
EAST KENT

East Kent is a wonderfully diverse landscape; natural waterways and wetlands, rolling downland, broad arable fields, orchards, woodlands and dramatic cliff top seascapes.

Stretching from Canterbury across to Thanet and Dover this area has been the setting for some of our most important historical events, providing the backdrop to invasions and celebrations, bearing witness to some of the country's darkest moments and greatest triumphs.

Visit Natural East Kent and discover our rich heritage and vibrant culture. The area is well served by three mainline rail lines and good bus links and there are plenty of cycling and walking trails.

www.nek.org.uk

Kent
County
Council

EAST SUSSEX

Places to Eat

Coriander Restaurant

5 Hove Manor, Hove Street, Hove,
East Sussex BN3 2DF

T: *+44 (0) 1273 730 850*

W: *www.corianderbrighton.com*

The majority of dishes on Coriander's menu are organic. They cross Latin with North African flavours including fish and meat dishes. Wild fish comes from sustainable sources and ingredients are local where possible. The restaurant is working hard to reduce its waste and focuses on recycling and uses natural cleaning products.

Earth & Stars Pub

46 Windsor Street, Brighton,
East Sussex BN1 1RJ

T: *+44 (0) 1273 722 879*

Earth and Stars may look like a regular pub, but the last few years have seen dedication to green causes including the installation of solar panelling and replacing branded products with organic and environmentally friendly beverages. There's a relaxed atmosphere and a healthy, organic menu.

Terre à Terre

71 East Street, Brighton, East Sussex BN1 1HQ

T: *+44 (0) 1273 729 051*

W: *www.terreaterre.co.uk*

You don't have to be vegetarian to lap up the expanse of flavours on offer at Terre à Terre. The food is adventurous and flavoursome with menu suggestions such as Iddli Spice Puff Cakes and Bad Boy Brinjal which consists of chunky charred aubergine bringal, served with coconut cumin curry leaf chatni. The wine and many of the spirits are organic with an increasing number of biodynamic varieties.

The Sanctuary Café

51-55 Brunswick Street East, Hove,
East Sussex BN3 1AU

T: *+44 (0) 1273 770 002*

W: *www.sanctuarycafe.co.uk*

The Sanctuary has been a long-standing favourite among vegetarians in Hove. The Café serves vegetarian, vegan and seafood dishes as well as bagels, salads, and a selection of cakes and speciality beverages including organic wines and beers. It's an arty place with regular exhibitions and music to relax to. Ingredients are sourced locally and the café supports fairtrade.

Miso Pretty dish at Terre à Terre, Brighton

Places to Visit

Middle Farm

Middle Farm, Firle, Lewes, East Sussex BN8 6LJ

T: *+44 (0) 1323 811 411*

W: *www.middlefarm.com*

Middle Farm lies at the foot of the South Downs. Sixth generation farmers run the 625-acre farm and are passionate about good quality British produce achieved through respecting the environment and looking after the animals. Visitors can see the working farm in action and meet the friendly chickens, ducks, spotted pigs and donkeys. The farm shops and restaurant serve every imaginable type of British food and drink including the UK's National Collection of Cider and Perry featuring the farm's own Pookhill Cider.

Places to Stay – Hotels, Self-Catering & B&Bs

Beachy Head Holiday Cottages

The Dipperays, East Dean,
East Sussex BN20 0BS

T: *+44 (0) 1323 423 878*

W: *www.beachyhead.org.uk*

Beachy Head looks out over the stunning South Downs AONB and is just minutes from the sea through adjoining fields. The **SILVER** cottages are converted 18th Century farm buildings each with their own character and charm. A tea room and farm shop selling the farm's own produce opened in 2007 to go alongside its micro brewery and Sheep Centre – one of the largest collections of rare sheep in the world. Walking and cycling opportunities are encouraged by the owners of Beachy Head who will be more than happy to point out the area's capacity for outdoor adventure. **For more insight into ecoescape 13 see pages 50-51.**

Beech Hill Farm

Rushlake Green, Heathfield,
East Sussex TN21 9QB
T: *+44 (0) 1435 830 203*
W: *www.sussexcountryretreat.co.uk*

The self-catering accommodation at Beech Hill Farm consists of the Coach House and the Studio Sanctuary which have both been carefully put together to offer guests responsible escapism in an environment which encourages creative expression. The organic farm is home to a flock of rare breed Black Wensleydale sheep which provide inspiration at any time of the year, particularly in spring. The open plan Coach House is a quaint but fully equipped 18th Century cottage while the Studio features chestnut flooring along with natural acoustics.

Blanch House

17 Atlingworth Street, Brighton,
East Sussex BN2 1PL
T: *+44 (0) 1273 603 504*
W: *www.blanchhouse.co.uk*

Owned by husband and wife Chris Edwardes and Amanda Blanch, Blanch House opened in 2000 and combines excellent service with innovative design in a laid back atmosphere. Their aim was to create a small, friendly hotel with a big personality. Located in a discreet Georgian terrace, just off Brighton's seafront, the grade II listed building offers 12 ensuite rooms together with a lounge-chic cocktail bar and an in-house restaurant serving mainly organic food, sourced locally where possible.

Brighton House

52 Regency Square, Brighton,
East Sussex BN1 2FF
T: *+44 (0) 1273 323 282*
W: *www.brighton-house.co.uk*

Rather than the traditional fry up, Brighton House serves up a lavish continental breakfast comprising wild and organic ingredients. Their rooms are unfussy and uncompromising on environmental awareness having reduced waste and energy consumption along with a host other small but significant measures. Being only five minutes away from the sea means that you are never far from the life and soul of the town. A recent extension has offered up more green space and energy savings with the addition of a sedum roof made with low growing plants.

Brightonwave

10 Madeira Place, Brighton,
East Sussex BN2 1TN
T: *+44 (0) 1273 676 794*
W: *www.brightonwave.com*

Brightonwave is a stylish hotel near to Brighton seafront. Here late breakfasts are positively encouraged to fully appreciate the owner's efforts to ensure all his guests leave calmed by his attentive service and impeccable taste. The hotel's reputation on the green scene is growing and its determination to reduce and recycle goes blissfully unnoticed by the hotel's contented guests.

Little Marshfoot

Mill Road, Hailsham, East Sussex BN27 2SJ
T: *+44 (0) 1323 844 690*
W: *www.littlemarshfoot.co.uk*

Little Marshfoot demonstrates that eco-living is 'no big deal' by offering its guests comfort and escapism in self-catering accomodation that puts the environment first. The lodge is situated in the grounds of a former farmhouse on the edge of the Pevensey Levels, an area that has a strong focus on conservation. Little Marshfoot is constructed of wood from sustainable sources in the UK, and is insulated with a product made from recycled telephone directories and newspapers. It has a covered loggia along the outside of the building with a large patio which together provide a peaceful outside space to enjoy the organic garden. **For more insight into ecoescape 14 see pages 52-53.**

Paskins Townhouse

18/19 Charlotte Street, Brighton,
East Sussex BN2 1AG
T: *+44 (0) 1273 601 203*
W: *www.paskins.co.uk*

Paskins has resolutely cast aside ordinariness in favour of its own values. This place is stylish and genuinely 'green' in outlook. It's just yards from the beach and close to the centre of things. There are 19 attractive rooms, with the odd four-poster bed. Breakfast, taken in a memorable art deco room includes a varied menu of organic and vegetarian food. **For more insight into ecoescape 15 see pages 54-55.**

HAMPSHIRE

Activities

Country Lanes New Forest

The Railway Station, Brockenhurst,
Hampshire SO42 7TW
T: +44 (0) 1590 622 627
W: www.countrylanes.co.uk

Explore the New Forest National Park by bicycle. Hire a bike at Brockenhurst railway station and follow one of the many routes through the forest. Country Lanes provides the bike hire and offers suggestions of trails to follow including child-friendly options and bicycles. **For more insight into ecoescape 19 see pages 62-63.**

Places to Stay – Hotels, Self-Catering & B&Bs

Scotland Farm Bed & Breakfast

Scotland Farm, Hawkley, Hampshire GU33 6NH
T: +44 (0) 1703 827 473
W: www.scotlandfarm.com

GOLD Less than an hour from London, Scotland Farm is a good choice for city escapists. Hilary, the owner, protects the natural habitats around the property managing the ancient woodland and restoration of the pond. This means that guests can enjoy walks around the farm during their stay. The rooms are situated around a courtyard with views out to the countryside.

Wetherdown Hostel

Droxford Road, East Meon, Petersfield,
Hampshire GU32 1HR
T: +44 (0) 1703 823 166
W: www.earthworks-trust.com

Wetherdown Hostel is attached to the Sustainability Centre on the South Downs. The hostel has been renovated using sustainable building materials and boasts an integrated solar photovoltaic roof and a wood chip biomass boiler. Some 50 tonnes of seasoned wood fuel per year are sourced from the site and from local sustainable woodland management. Earth Works Trust, the charity running the Centre and hostel was set up to provide an on-location facility to prove that green principles can be applied to all aspects of business, education and leisure. Tipis and yurts are also available to hire on the hostel's secluded camping ground.

Cyclists at Sandy Balls Holiday Park, Hampshire

Places to Stay – Campsites & Holiday Parks

Sandy Balls

Godshill, Fordingbridge, Hampshire SP6 2JZ
T: +44 (0) 1425 653 042
W: www.sandy-balls.co.uk

GOLD Sandy Balls is located deep in the New Forest. Here you can stay in lodges nestled in 120-acres of woodland. The site has a prestigious David Bellamy Gold Conservation Award to its name and provides a number of nature walks for its guests. There's also a solar heated swimming pool, electric site vehicles and waste segregation initiatives.

ISLE OF WIGHT

Places to Stay – Hotels, Self-Catering & B&Bs

Hobbit House
Whitwell, Ventnor,
Isle of Wight PO38 2QQ
T: +44 (0) 1983 731 514
W: www.hobbithouse.co.uk
Hobbit House B&B is run with sensitivity to the surrounding countryside and wildlife. As well as offering guests a tranquil rural retreat, owners Oswald and Julie also give one-to-one coaching sessions in countryside skills and woodland crafts like hedgelaying and charcoal making. Their eco-friendly transport comes in the form of horse drawn carriage and they will come out anywhere on the island to collect guests.

KENT

Places to Eat

The Goods Shed
Station Road West, Canterbury,
Kent CT2 8AN
T: +44 (0) 1227 459 153
Moving from industry to edibles, this former coal depot is now Canterbury's famous permanent farmer's market. The bakery, butchery and market together supply the restaurant with fresh produce and a fair deal for Kent producers. The unique setting and excellent menu are a real draw for diners looking for a complete gastro experience.

Places to Visit

Brogdale Horticultural Trust
Brogdale Road, Faversham,
Kent ME13 8XZ
T: +44 (0) 1795 535 286
W: www.brogdale.org
Brogdale is home of the National Fruit Collection, a natural gallery of colour and taste responsible for preserving the genetic diversity of England's cultivated fruit. The Apple Collection is thought to be the largest in the world and incorporates both new and established varieties some dating back to the reign of Henry VIII. Guided tours around the collections by Brogdale's famous pomologist take place daily which are an opportunity to marvel at the huge variety growing in the orchards and

sample some of the country's most delicious pickings. Award winning fruit juice and cider is on hand to quench your thirst and there is plenty of local produce available in the farm shop.

Apples at Brogdale Horticultural Trust, Kent

Garden Organic Yalding
Benover Road, Yalding,
Near Maidstone, Kent ME18 6EX
T: +44 (0) 1622 814 650
W: www.gardenorganic.org.uk
You know by now that ale is a common theme in ecoescape. We jump at any chance to try the local brew. In Kent there are plenty of opportunities as well as plenty of hop growers to supply the local breweries. Garden Organic in Yalding is in the heart of all this and has a back drop of hop gardens and oast houses. Even the pergola is made from recycled hop poles. The organic gardens tell the story of gardening through the ages in 18 themed display areas.

Rippledown Environmental Education Centre
Ripple Down House, Dover Road,
Ringwould, Deal, Kent CT14 8HE
T: +44 (0) 1304 364 854
W: www.rippledown.com
'Knowledge through nature' is the philosophy behind Rippledown. The three-acres are used for fieldwork including pond sampling, minibeast and nature trails, as well as artwork and environmental recording. Studies can be linked to their website

and Biowatch – an environmental monitoring programme set up to record biodiversity, seasonal change and the local environment.

Romney Marsh Visitor Centre

Dymchurch Road, New Romney,
Kent TN28 8AY

T: *+44 (0) 1797 369 487*
W: *www.rhdr.org.uk*

Romney Marsh is a 100-square-mile area of wetlands in Kent and East Sussex. The visitor centre in the country park houses information and exhibitions on the wildlife and history of the marshes. The building itself uses straw bales as walls and insulation, and is topped with a living roof. The Centre is open during the weekends.

Activities

Walk Awhile

Montgreenan, St. Catherines Drive,
Faversham, Kent ME13 8QL

T: *+44 (0) 1227 752 762*
W: *www.walkawhile.co.uk*

Under the watchful eye of local man Derek Bright, Walk Awhile offers tailor made walking tours of the Kent Downs Area of **SILVER** Outstanding Natural Beauty. If you choose a self-led tour, you will be seen off armed with a map, itinerary and list of local businesses along the way for sustenance and more local knowledge, before being reunited again with your luggage at your next accommodation. Derek's signature guided walk of the Pilgrim's Way between the cities of Rochester and Canterbury encompasses a six day amble through the North Downs stopping off at bewitching little villages and historical sites such as the splendid Leeds Castle. **For more insight into ecoescape 17 see pages 58 – 59.**

Places to Stay – Hotels, Self-Catering & B&Bs

Alkham Court

Meggett Lane, South Alkham,
Dover, Kent CT15 7DG

T: *+44 (0) 1303 892 056*
W: *www.alkhamcourt.co.uk*

Alkham Court enjoys stunning views across the valley onto land farmed by Wendy and Neil, the owners of this **GOLD** comfortable bed and breakfast. The farm is managed to a high standard of environmental protection including the introduction of a wild flower meadow. The possibilities for walking are too tempting to miss and the farm is a great

starting point following the sheep and horses across the hills. There are numerous recycling and energy saving initiatives at the B&B and the Burrows would be more than happy to share the warmth of their open fire.

Brenley Farm

Brenley Lane, Boughton,
Faversham, Kent ME13 9LY

T: *+44 (0) 1227 751 203*
W: *www.brenley-farm.co.uk*

Close to the market town of Faversham, Brenley Farm is a rural retreat on a traditional Kentish working farm. The **SILVER** grounds contain apple and pear orchards as well as a small acreage of hops which help supply the local Shepherd Neame brewery. The breakfast menu changes daily depending on availability from the farm and surrounding area. **For more insight into ecoescape 16 see pages 56-57.**

Iffin House

Iffin Lane, Canterbury,
Kent CT4 7BE

T: *+44 (0) 1227 462 776*
W: *www.iffinfarmhouse.co.uk*

Iffin House and its surrounding apple orchards contain stories from a bygone era of English country living which never **BRONZE** fails to captivate its guests. Food miles are kept to a minimum by sourcing the next door neighbour's eggs, jams and Kentish apple juice. The rest is grown in their grounds and prepared on a wood burning stove. There are also facilities for meetings and conferencing in an inspiring location. 'Thinking space' can be found in the cute self catering cabin at the end of the garden in the Orchard Pickers Cottage.

Palace Farm

Doddington, Sittingbourne,
Kent ME9 0AU

T: *+44 (0) 1795 886 200*
W: *www.palacefarm.com*

Palace Farm combines hostel accommodation with B&B service and comfort. Cyclists will love the facilities **GOLD** available including cycle hire and a drying room. Nothing goes to waste at this hostel. The wood burning stove inside the modern kitchen uses excess wood from the farm as fuel. Water is heated by solar panelling and all of the plant pots had previous lives as potato bulk bins. The farm has set itself a carbon neutral target incorporating plans for more renewable sources of energy. The range of products harvested at the farm throughout the calendar includes an unlikely combination of strawberries, wheat, pumpkins and Christmas trees.

Wallett's Court Hotel

Westcliffe, Dover, Kent CT15 6EW
T: +44 (0) 1304 852 424
W: *www.wallettscourthotel.com*

Wallett's Court is a grand country house hotel near to the famous White Cliffs. The bedrooms in the hotel feature four poster beds fit for royalty. Just across the courtyard fourteen further rooms are housed in Kentish hay barns, stables and cow sheds. The restaurant uses local and seasonal produce and has developed a reputation for fine dining and gastronomic flare. The hotel uses its own well water and is currently investing in alternative energy generation methods.

Willow Farm Bed and Breakfast

Willow Farm, Stone Cross, Bilsington, Ashford, Kent TN25 7JJ
T: +44 (0) 1233 721 700
W: *www.willowfarmenterprises.co.uk*

Willow Farm B&B is located on an organic smallholding in quiet rural Kent, close to the Eurostar terminal in Ashford. The owners have planted hundreds of trees since moving to the farm in 1985 and created several conservation areas including two new ponds. Home-made organic bread is served for breakfast in the farmhouse kitchen.

LONDON

Places to Eat

Acorn House

69 Swinton Street, Clerkenwell, London WC1X 9NT
T: +44 (0) 207 812 1842
W: *www.acornhouserestaurant.com*

Acorn House opened in 2006 amid claims to be the UK's first training restaurant to focus on sustainable principles. The restaurant director and head chef combine their long and inspiring culinary careers with the potential to make a real difference in the promotion of healthy eating, reduction of waste and championing British produce.

Blah Blah Blah

78 Goldhawk Road, London W12 HA
T: +44 (0) 20 8746 1337

Bring a bottle and your appetite to the Blah Blah

The hostel at Palace Farm, Kent

Blah vegetarian restaurant near Shepherds Bush. Food is modern and imaginative, as well as affordable. The dishes are kept simple to reward customers with great quality and immaculate presentation.

Daylesford Organic Café

The Old Bank, 31 Sloane Square, London SW1 8AG
T: +44 (0) 20 7881 8020
W: *www.daylesfordorganic.com*

The Daylesford Organic Café in Sloane Square opened in 2005 and brought a taste of Daylesford to the capital. Homemade soups, cheeses, salads, light lunches and teas are served daily, with speciality coffees, teas, freshly squeezed juices and smoothies. Menus feature organic ingredients whenever possible and change regularly according to the season.

Farm W5

19 The Green, Ealing, London W5 5DA
T: +44 (0) 20 8566 1965
W: *www.farmw5.com*

Endorsed by the Slow Food Movement, Farm W5 is an organic and artisan food market located in West London. The deli area features over 50 hand-picked cheeses and a range of cooked meats from around the UK. At the back of the market there is a coffee shop and organic juice bar serving healthy foods to help you de-tox.

Freightliners Farm

Sheringham Road, London N7 8PF
T: +44 (0) 207 609 0467
W: *www.freightlinersfarm.org.uk*

Freightliners Farm was founded on wasteland behind Kings Cross station in London in 1973. Originally the animals were housed in railway goods vans, hence the name. The Farm moved to its present site in 1978 and new purpose built farm buildings were erected in 1988. Visitors can get to know the animals and eat at the café built using straw bales and green oak.

Konstam at the Prince Albert

2 Acton Street, London WC 1X 9NA

T: +44 (0) 207 833 5040

W: www.konstam.co.uk

The Konstam at the Prince Albert sources all its ingredients from within the M25. The open plan kitchen serves up fish from the Thames and steak from Sevenoakes along with seasonal produce and a range of English wine. The restaurant itself is a welcoming mix of traditional London pub and modern decor.

Leon Restaurants

35 Great Marlborough Street, London W 1F 7JE

T: +44 (0) 20 7437 5280

W: www.leonrestaurants.co.uk

Leon restaurants serve fresh, seasonal fast food, combining the speed and modest pricing of a fast food outlet with high-quality, flavour-packed food. Serving breakfast, lunch and supper (from the take away counter, or to eat in) Leon is committed to seasonality with ingredients from trusted farms and flavoured with natural herbs and spices.

Mildred's Restaurant

45 Lexington Street, Soho, London W 1F 9AN

T: +44 (0) 20 7494 1634

W: www.mildreds.co.uk

A busy veggie eatery that by its nature and Soho location demands informality and a relaxed outlook from its customers. That said the dishes are prepared with a strong ethos toward seasonal and organic produce. Dishes are world-inspired and include gyoza, Malaysian curry and mediterranean ratatouille. There is also a selection of organic wines and beers.

The Duke of Cambridge

30 St Peters Street, Islington, London N 1 8JT

T: +44 (0) 20 7359 3066

W: www.dukeorganic.co.uk

The Duke of Cambridge is the UK's first and only Soil Association-certified organic pub. Originally built in 1851, the pub has been restored using reclaimed building materials while retaining many original features. Waste is recycled including food waste for compost and all the ingredients are local wherever possible, as well as organic. The menu changes twice a day, and all the organic beers are from small artisan breweries and the 50 strong wine list is all organic.

The Gate

51 Queen Caroline Street, London W6 9QL

T: +44 (0) 20 8748 6932

W: www.thegate.tv

Adrian Daniel confounded family members when he announced at the age of 17 his conversion to vegetarianism. His brother Michael had faith in the idea and later co-founded the Gate vegetarian restaurant with him in 1989. Since then it has earned a reputation for serving fresh and tasty dishes with gluten-free and vegan options like the Three Artichoke Salad or Trumpet and Root Vegetable Ragu. To accompany, there is a wide selection of organic wine.

The Place Below

St Mary-le-Bow Church, Cheapside, London EC 2V AU

T: +44 (0) 20 7329 0789

W: www.theplacebelow.co.uk

If you think church refectory means milky tea and custard creams, you should really experience one of Bill Swell's trinity of church-based restaurants. The Place Below is buried in the crypt of St Mary Le Bow in the City of London. Here Bill's team serves home-made vegetarian breakfasts and lunches including much-loved quiches, sandwiches and tasty cakes all made from seasonal and local ingredients.

Water House Restaurant

10 Orsman Road, London N 1 5QJ

T: +44 (0) 207 033 0123

W: www.waterhouserestaurant.co.uk

As if Acorn House in London wasn't green enough, the people behind London's first sustainable restaurant recently went one step further with the opening of Water House Restaurant in North London. The canalside restaurant uses only hydro electric power for electricity and the ambient water temperature of the canal to provide a cooling and heating system for the building. Water House uses only fresh, seasonal and organic produce, and all waste is digested in wormeries and a hot composter in the restaurant's community garden.

Wild Cherry

241-245 Globe Road, Bethnal Green, London E 2 0JD

T: +44 (0) 20 8980 6678

In a busy corner of London's East End, Wild Cherry serves vegan and vegetarian dishes brimming with international flavours. The café's relaxed atmosphere is helped on by the friendly team of Buddhist ladies who plough all profits back into meditation teaching at the London Buddhist

Centre next door. The restorative powers of their breakfasts is a good opportunity to sample one of the most popular fry-ups in Bethnal Green.

Places to Visit

Islington Ecology Centre

Gillespie Park Local Nature Reserve, 191 Drayton Park, London N5 1PH
T: *+44 (0) 20 7354 5162*
W: *www.islington.gov.uk*

Passengers in and out of King's Cross station are able to view the Islington Ecology Centre found in Gillespie Park Nature Reserve. The local wildlife was welcomed back to the area in the early eighties when wasteland was designated for park use. During the following decade the Ecology Centre was added to this to create a platform for sustainability and learning. The exhibition in the centre focuses on its contribution to the local wildlife and the building itself has a host of sustainable features including solar panelling and reed bed water recycling.

London Wetland Centre

Queen Elizabeth's Walk, Barnes, London SW13 9WT
T: *+44 (0) 20 8409 4400*
W: *www.wwt.org.uk*

The city horizon seems a thousand miles from the wetland landscape in Barnes, which is in fact just as close to the heart of the capital. Wild birds find a haven to nest and feed at the Wetland Centre, or to stop over on their long migratory journeys. Visitors can watch them from the purpose-built hides and discover other types of species like butterflies and moths. Life in the wetlands is examined in finer detail through the exhibits and interactive discovery centre. **For more insight into ecoescape 12 see pages 48-49.**

Natural History Museum

Cromwell Road, London, London SW7 5BD
T: *+44 (0) 20 7942 5000*
W: *www.nhm.ac.uk*

Find out the real reason dinosaurs died out and absorb yourself with nature on a grand scale at the Natural History Museum. Starting in the magnificent Central Hall, the 1,300-year old Sequoia tree is today the biggest living thing and is an impressive display of nature over time. Elsewhere other exhibits help visitors to connect with nature for the survival of the planet. Highlights include a walk-in 'leaf factory' in the Ecology Zone and a photographic display of the

power of plants to find out how plants are used to make things like cosmetics and toiletries.

Activities

London Bicycle Tour Company

1a Gabriels Wharf, 56 Upper Ground, London SE1 9PP
T: *+44 (0) 20 7928 6838*
W: *www.londonbicycle.com*

Forget open-top buses, the best way to see London is by bicycle. However, if the idea of navigating the capital's busy streets by bicycle feels you with fear, the London Bicycle Tour Company can step in and escort your group to see some of London's best views. The company supplies the bicycles and the guides and will tailor rides according to time and location including destinations in the South East and East Anglia as well as central London.

London Pedicabs

No.1 Molines Wharf, 98-100 Narrow Street, London E14 8BP
T: *+44 (0) 207 093 3155*
W: *www.londonpedicabs.com*

London's pedicabs can be seen out and about in London's West End taking customers between theatres, restaurants and tube stations. The drivers are vetted and can act as a local tour guide or just help you get from A to B.

Places to Stay – Hotels, Self-Catering & B&Bs

Apex City of London Hotel

No 1 Seething Lane, London, London EC3N 4AX
T: *+44 (0) 207 702 2020*
W: *www.apexhotels.co.uk*

Located at the heart of London's financial district, the Apex City of London Hotel proves that environmental concern is best for the bottom line. The Scotland based hotel group has its own architect specialising in sustainable hotel design and this recent modern build incorporates a string of environmentally friendly design features. The rooms are modern without being corporate and many enjoy views of Tower Bridge.

One Aldwych

1 Aldwych, London WC2B 4RH
T: *+44 (0) 207 300 1000*
W: *www.onealdwych.co.uk*

With its finger tightly on the pulse, One Aldwych occupies an enviable position in London's West End. Accommodation is slick, contemporary and unobtrusive. The staff are not only attentive to their customers but also to the planet. From day one they are introduced to the hotel's Green Team before being sent off with a handful of seeds to plant a tree. Guests can choose between a tempting selection of in-house bars and restaurants which endeavour to promote home grown produce in their 'Taste Britain' menu. The hotel works a successful behind-the-scenes environmental policy.

The Zetter
St John's Square, 86-88 Clerkenwell Road, London EC1M 5RJ
T: *+44 (0) 207 324 4444*
W: *www.thezetter.com*

The Zetter is a boutique hotel in the Clerkenwell area of London. The decor mixes retro with city style, and the rooms, although some quite small, speak good taste and thoughtful design. The hotel is in a converted warehouse and uses FSC-certified timber from sustainable sources. It is independent of mains water as the supply comes from deep below the ground via the hotel's own pump and borehole. **For more insight into ecoescape** see pages 46-47.

SURREY

Places to Visit

Royal Botanic Gardens Kew
Kew, Richmond, Surrey TW9 3AB
T: *+44 (0) 20 8332 5655*
W: *www.kew.org*

There are over 300 acres of plant and tree life in which to lose yourself at Kew Gardens. The arboretums, glass houses and gardens are a constantly changing mosaic of colour and scents. They are helping to conserve thousands of species of plants from around the world, from Himalayan rhododendrons to native English woodland covered in bluebells. Visitors can explore ten climatic zones transporting them to steamy rainforests as well as arid deserts. Kew also takes great care in reducing its waste and reusing water for feeding the plants.

Sutton Ecology Centre
Festival Walk, Carshalton, Surrey SM5 3NY
T: *+44 (0) 20 8770 5820*
W: *www.sutton.gov.uk*

A green space for urbanites, Sutton Ecology Centre is a place to get some hands-on experience of the environment. Holiday activities range from wood carving to wreath making with the backdrop of meadows, ponds, woodlands and organic gardens. A sensory garden makes full uses of your faculties with its grass textures, colourful flowers and sweet-smelling herbs.

Sunday lunch at the Duke of Cambridge, London

Asperion Hotel

73 Farnham Road, Guildford, Surrey GU2 7PF
T: *+44 (0) 1483 579 299*
W: *www.asperion-hotel.co.uk*

SILVER The Asperion Hotel's recent renovations have engaged uncompromisingly with supporting the environment and fairtrade. The proprietor is all out to improve the local organic supply chain to ensure that the Asperion can offer its guests a 100% organic menu. Contemporary chic along with the tasteful side of squeaky clean service has already earned this hotel a reputation among pleasure seekers and business travellers alike. The hotel caters for disabled guests and offers wellbeing packages in conjunction with a top local spa.

WEST SUSSEX

Canute Cottages

Chidham, Chichester, West Sussex PO18 8TE
T: *+44 (0) 1243 572 123*
W: *www.canutecottages.co.uk*

GOLD Canute Cottages are grouped around an old farm courtyard with a private water frontage onto Chichester Harbour. The Beale family and their guests have long benefited from the proximity to the sea but have ensured that its natural beauty is maintained through their local harbour conservancy trust. A resident flock of Jacob's Sheep have helped realise a 14-year project to turn arable land back into precious coastal grazing fields and marsh. Meanwhile guests can enjoy dinghy sailing and· their very own leisure barn jam packed full of traditional games for rainy days.

Old Chapel Forge

Lagness, Chichester , West Sussex PO20 1LR
T: *+44 (0) 1243 264 380*
W: *www.oldchapelforge.co.uk*

GOLD Old Chapel Forge B&B has acquired local green celebrity status for its dedication to reducing the impact of every aspect of its business from solar panel heated water and grey water recycling to providing food produced by local farmers. The history of the house and chapel dates as far back as 1611. **For more insight into ecoscape 18 see pages 60-61.**

St Martin's Organic Tearooms

3 St Martin's Street, Chichester,
West Sussex PO19 1NP
T: *+44 (0) 1243 786 715*
W: *www.organictearooms.co.uk*

St Martin's is a certified organic tearooms in the centre of Chichester. It's full of historic appeal due to its medieval building, log fires and beamed interiors. There are also two secluded gardens for al fresco dining and outside music renditions. The food served at St Martins is home-made and super healthy but also full of flavour. Specials include Spinach and Apple Potato Cake and Welsh Rarebit.

East Anglia

*Waffles topped with maple syrup at
the Waffle House, Norwich
– see page 166*

*Backpackers' Hostel at Deepdale Farm, Norfolk –
see page 168*

*The solar boat Ra on the Broads, Norfolk
© Broads Authority – see page 167*

East Anglia

GO SLOW
IN EAST ANGLIA

As a Suffolk-born girl who now lives in the city, I'm at liberty to say that East Anglia generally feels like a slow place to be in. Much of the landscape is rural which means that people's daily rhythms are naturally different to those in other areas of the UK. There are also many sleepy villages with age-old buildings and the sea-air stemming from miles of coastline is inevitably a de-accelerator on activity. There are still some rural railway stations meaning that getting out into the countryside isn't a difficult task. Flat landscapes also mean that the terrain is ideal for Sunday cyclists.

SLOW TRAVEL OPTIONS

Boating on the Broads
W: *www.broads-authority.gov.uk*
Narrow boats aren't known for their speed so boating on the Broads is a fine example of a slow holiday. There are thousands of waterways across the UK (see www.waterscape.com) but the Broads enjoys over 125 miles of waterways in Norfolk and Suffolk and is in itself a National Park. You can hire a narrow boat for the duration of your holiday or take a trip out on one of the specialist boats, like Ra – a solar-powered boat from Gay's Staithe in Neatishead.

Norfolk Green Buses
W: *www.norfolkgreen.co.uk*
The buses of Norfolk Green cover 80 miles of routes across Norfolk, Cambridgeshire and Lincolnshire. The Coasthopper bus links up seaside villages on the North Norfolk coast including Sheringham, Cley-next-to-the-Sea and Brancaster Staithe.

The Bittern Line
W: *www.bitternline.com*
Another way to see the experience the Norfolk Broads is to hop on the Bittern railway line which runs from Norwich to the North Norfolk coastal towns of Cromer and Sheringham. The journey stops off a various points on the Broads and cycles can be carried on the train (reservations are recommended).

ESSEX

Places to Visit

Audley End Organic Kitchen Garden
Saffron Walden, Essex CB11 4JF
T: *+44 (0) 1799 522 399*
W: *www.hdra.org.uk*
The Kitchen Garden at Audley End not only looks like a garden from the Victorian era but is also managed in a similar way to the Victorians at a time when there were no synthetic pesticides available. Inspired by their techniques of organic growing, the gardens at Audley End are a menagerie of vines, fruit trees and vegetables. The Vine House was built in 1804 and contains grapevines planted in 1917.

Rainham Marshes RSPB
New Tank Hill Road, Purfleet, Essex RM19 1SZ
T: *+44 (0) 1708 899 840*
W: *www.rspb.org.uk/rainham*
On ancient marshland to the East of London, Rainham Marshes was saved from development by the RSPB and local campaigners in 2000. Today the wetland expanse is home to a diverse bird population including wading birds, finches and birds of prey. The Environment and Education centre provides views across the marshes and River Thames, as well as containing a café, shop and classroom. The building uses solar panels, rainwater harvesting, natural light and ventilation and has a ground source heat exchange system.

NORFOLK

Places to Eat

The Waffle House
39 St Giles Street, Norwich, Norfolk NR2 1JN
T: *+44 (0) 1603 612 790*
W: *www.wafflehouse.co.uk*
The Waffle House is a good choice for a filling lunch in the centre of Norwich. The delectable range of sweet and savoury waffles covers all toppings from fairtrade banoffee and hot Dutch apple to roasted red peppers and hummus and avocado. The flour used in the waffles is organically grown and stone-ground at the local Redbournbury Mill.

Places to Visit

Bewilderwood

Horning Road, Hoveton, Wroxham,
Norfolk NR12 8JW
T: *+44 (0) 1603 783 900*
W: *www.bewilderwood.co.uk*

The 'deli' of theme parks, Bewilderwood is an adventure through the make-believe world of Boggles and Twiggles. Their tale is told through the pages of a story book and brought to life at Bewilderwood on the Norfolk Broads. Tom Blofeld, Bewilderwood's founder, made sure that the theme park not only would encourage children's imaginations but also be as sustainable as possible. Visitors are requested not to upset the Twiggles by dropping litter or harming the wildlife and the wood used for the tree houses comes from a sustainable source. **For more insight into ecoescape 20 see pages 64-65.**

Brancaster Millennium Activity Centre

Dial House, Brancaster Staithe,
Kings Lynn, Norfolk PE13 8BW
T: *+44 (0) 1485 210 719*
W: *www.nationaltrust.org/brancaster*

Coastal-inspired Brancaster Millennium Activity Centre is an environmental education centre located in the Norfolk fishing village of Brancaster Staithe. Sustainable materials were used for the renovation of this 17th Century building and by embracing renewable energy in the centre's day to day running, visitors are able to learn about sustainable living in this important coastal zone. The building draws heat from the mud flats using a heat-exchange system, along with the assistance of solar energy and wind-power to provide top-up energy sources. The National Trust has ensured that not only the building itself continues to be an example of sustainable living, but equally the surrounding saltmarshes, sand dunes and creeks remain picture perfect and inhabitable for wildlife.

Ecotech Centre

Turbine Way, Swaffham, Norfolk PE37 7HT
T: *+44 (0) 1760 726 100*
W: *www.ecotech.org.uk*

The wind turbine at the Ecotech Centre, otherwise known as Swaffham-I, provides enough electricity to power over 1,000 homes, an emission saving of over 3,161 tonnes of CO2 per year. The turbine also hides a spiral stairway up to the public viewing platform designed by Foster & Partners. Turbine tours are available by visiting the Ecotech Centre; a hub for environmental education welcoming delegations of adults and children alike. Admission to the centre is free; however turbine tours are chargeable but well worth the 305-stair climb. **For more insight into ecoescape 23 see pages 70-71.**

Activities

Ra Solar Boat

Gay's Staithe, Neatishead, Norfolk
T: *+44 (0) 1603 782 281*
W: *www.broads-authority.gov.uk*

The world's first solar-powered passenger boat named after the Egyptian sun god, Ra, has been ferrying sun worshippers on the Norfolk Broads since 2000. She traverses the waterways of the nature reserve silently storing power in the seven rows of panels overhead and providing passengers with the opportunity to view the restoration taking place on the Barton Broads, only possible by boat. Ra can carry up to 12 passengers and boards in Gay's Staithe in Neatishead.

Places to Stay – Hotels, Self-Catering & B&Bs

Pinetrees

Park Drive, Beccles, Norfolk NR34 7DQ
T: *+44 (0) 1502 470 796*
W: *www.pinetrees.net*

Pinetrees is a purpose built sustainable B&B in the pretty town of Beccles. The building, which sits on a wildflower meadow, was designed by a local architect and uses wood from sustainable sources. Water is heated by solar panelling and rainwater is collected for toilet flushing and washing laundry. The building also benefits from a biological sewage processor. A fairtrade breakfast is on offer with eggs gathered from the garden. Guests arriving by foot or by bicycle receive a generous discount. **For more insight into ecoescape 22 see pages 68-69.**

Strattons Hotel

4 Ash Close, Swaffham, Norfolk PE37 7NH
T: *+44 (0) 1760 723 845*
W: *www.strattonshotel.com*

Bold colours, fine dining, art around every corner; this is no ordinary hotel. Strattons treats its guests to uninhibited luxury with individually styled rooms. This listed villa abides by a rigorous environmental policy involving all its staff members and supporting the local community. The grounds contain an onsite recycling facility and fruit trees have been planted in every available space. The restaurant serves excellent local produce. **For more insight into ecoescape 21 see pages 66-67.**

Clippesby Hall

Clippesby, Norfolk NR29 3BL
T: *+44 (0) 1493 367 800*
W: *www.clippesby.com*

SILVER Close to the Norfolk Broads, the campsite at Clippesby Hall has a strong reputation for its commitment to the environment with a David Bellamy award for conservation. The onsite pub and shop serve local and fairtrade produce and customers can hire bicycles. The site contains some secluded spots as well as family areas and immaculate facilities. There are some wooden cabins onsite for those who prefer a roof overhead.

Deepdale Farm

Burnham Deepdale, , Norfolk PE31 8DD
T: *+44 (0) 1485 210 256*
W: *www.deepdalefarm.co.uk*

GOLD Deepdale Farm combines hostel and camping accommodation on the North Norfolk Coast. Tipis are also available to hire while the Granary Hostel sleeps 18 people in varied sized dorms. Solar panelling throughout the site heats water for washing and powers the slow but highly efficient under floor heating. Meanwhile the local wildlife and bird populations flourish through the careful planning of crop rotation and hedge growth.

SUFFOLK

Milden Hall

The Hall, Milden, Lavenham, Sudbury, Suffolk CO10 9NY
T: *+44 (0) 1787 247235*
W: *www.thehall-milden.co.uk*

The farmhouse at Milden Hall is a converted Tudor barn, able to accommodate more than 22 guests. Self-catering here has an entirely new meaning with the possibility to re-enact a medieval banquet. The barn boasts 95 feet in length and the Hawkins have come up with some noteworthy energy savings for this building and connecting cartlodge. The wood burning stove is fuelled by farm hedgerow coppiced wood. The flooring in the barn is natural coir based while the cartlodge benefits from under floor heating. B&B accommodation is also available in the magnificent hall. **For more insight into ecoescape 24 see pages 72-73.**

Camping at Clippesby Hall, Norfolk

the Midlands

An eco-day out at the Natural World Centre, Lincolnshire – see page 172

A green youth hostel in the National Forest, Derbyshire – see page 170

The Midlands

GO SLOW
IN THE MIDLANDS

The Peak District National Park gets busy in the summer months. Traffic can clog up roads quickly so I always arrive by bus or train. There's usually a campsite nearby to the station or otherwise you can bring a bicycle on the train and cycle to your accommodation. Elsewhere in the Midlands, take the train (www.eastmidlandstrains.com) or walk (www.nationaltrail.co.uk).

SLOW TRAVEL OPTIONS

Peak Connections
W: *www.visitpeakdistrict.com/html/travel*
Peak Connections is all about helping travellers to the National Park reconsider their travel habits to incorporate a slower, more sustainable way to travel. The tourist board has created some useful guides linking up popular attractions like Chatsworth House with bus routes across Derbyshire and the Peaks. The guides contain discounts and ideas to help you form itineraries for your trip starting in various locations. They can be downloaded from the website.

Transpeak
W: *www.transpeak.co.uk*
The Transpeak coach service runs between Nottingham, Derby and Manchester stopping at various locations the length of the Peak District. The luxury coaches are comfortable and a great place to enjoy the view.

Shropshire Shuttle
W: *www.shropshirehillsshuttles.co.uk*
The Shropshire Shuttle buses operate during weekends between April and October transporting visitors around the Shropshire Hills AONB. Buses call at the picturesque villages of Craven Arms, Church Stretton, and Clun.

DERBYSHIRE

Places to Eat

The Walnut Club
Unit 6 The Square, Main Road,
Hathersage, Derbyshire S32 1BB
T: *+44 (0) 1433 651 155*
W: *www.thewalnutclub.com*
A strictly organic restaurant featuring stylish dining in a rural setting. The combination works well for the head chef Nicholas Wilson who is pushing the restaurant to national acclaim. With plenty to offer vegetarians and vegans, this restaurant is all about slow dining and wholesome cuisine with dishes like Roasted Rib of Derbyshire Farm Assured Beef and Slow Roasted Crispy Pork with Gascon Cabbage.

Places to Stay – Hotels, Self-Catering & B&Bs

Beechenhill Farm
Ilam, Ashbourne, Derbyshire DE6 2BD
T: *+44 (0) 1335 310 274*
W: *www.beechenhill.co.uk*
An organic limestone farm located in the stunning Peak District National Park. Wake up to a wandering cow outside the window of the bed and breakfast before tucking into an organic dairy breakfast. The self-catering cottage is a cosy hideaway for up to six people. If you need spoiling, enjoy a home cooked meal of stew and dumplings from the farm before jumping into the hot tub with views over the Peak District. The owners are rich in environmental and local knowledge and have established a farm trail which follows a natural shelter belt of oaks, ashes and silver birch before meandering through woodland, meadows and around beehives.

YHA National Forest
48 Bath Lane, Moira, Swadlincote,
Derbyshire DE12 6BD
T: *0870 770 6141*
W: *www.yha.org.uk*
The National Forest is a work in progress as 200-square miles of central England is transformed to blend new and mature woodland within varying landscapes. Opened in 2008, the YHA in the National Forest treads lightly as it features solar-heated water, rainwater harvesting system and a woodchip boiler using wood from sustainable forests.

Places to Stay – Campsites & Holiday Parks

Bushey Heath Farm

Tideswell Moor, Tideswell, Buxton,
Derbyshire SK17 8JE

T: *+44 (0) 1298 873 007*
W: *www.busheyheathfarm.co.uk*

Bushey Heath Farm offers accommodation in the form of a bunk barn, bothys, camping and caravans. The farm is in the heart of the Peak District near to the pretty village of Tideswell. Rod, the farmer, generates energy for the farm using a wind turbine and a ground source heat pump provides the heating. **For more insight into ecoescape 27 see pages 78-79.**

General Organisations

Peak District Environmental Quality Mark

Peak District National Park Authority,
Aldern House, Baslow Road, Bakewell,
Derbyshire DE45 1AE

T: *+44 (0) 1629 816 321*
W: *www.peakdistrict.gov.uk/eqm*

The Peak District Environmental Quality Mark is a certification mark for businesses in the tourism industry. It can only be achieved by businesses that actively support good environmental practices in the Peak District National Park. When you buy a product or service that has been awarded the Mark you can be confident that your purchase directly supports the sustainable management of the environment in the Peak District National Park.

The cottage and view at Beechenhill Farm, Derbyshire

HEREFORDSHIRE

Places to Eat

Nature's Choice Restaurant & Guesthouse

Raglan House, 17 Broad Street,
Ross-on-Wye, Herefordshire HR9 7EA

T: *+44 (0) 1989 763 454*
W: *www.natures-choice.biz*

Nature's Choice is a licensed restaurant and guesthouse serving organic food with an American influence. The large selection of home-baked goods include many that are gluten-free, vegetarian and vegan. Recycling, conservation and community building are also a part of the 'big picture' at Nature's Choice.

Places to Stay – Hotels, Self-Catering & B&Bs

Aspen House

Hoarwithy, Herefordshire HR2 6QP

T: *+44 (0) 1432 840 353*
W: *www.aspenhouse.net*

Slow food advocates, Sally and Rob at Aspen House are so particular about the freshness of their eggs that they collect them fresh every day from a local farm, the only one in the area to meet their exacting standards. The house itself is a converted farm building and the grounds also contain a small but cosy self-catering cottage, once a cider mill. Energy saving is apparent throughout and the garden is free to be explored by guests. **For more insight into ecoescape 28 see pages 80-81.**

Penrhos Court Hotel & Restaurant

Penrhos, Kington, Herefordshire HR5 3LH

T: *+44 (0) 1544 230 720*
W: *www.penrhos.com; www.greencuisine.com*

Penrhos Court is a 700-year old manor farm on the border of Herefordshire and Wales . It has been rebuilt and is now devoted to food, health and ecology. It is home to the Greencuisine School of Food and Health which runs organic nutritional-based courses.

LEICESTERSHIRE

Places to Visit

Brocks Hill Environmental Centre
Washbrook Lane, Oadby, Leicester,
Leicestershire LE2 5JJ
T: +44 (0) 116 257 2888
W: *www.brockshill.co.uk*
The environmentally friendly visitor centre at
Brocks Hill sits amid a 30-hectare country park
featuring woods, orchards, wildflower meadows
and ponds. The Centre itself houses permanent and
visiting exhibitions covering everything from
energy efficient buildings to a people powered hair
dryer. The building incorporates a host of
environmental practices including rainwater
collection for toilet flushing, recycled newspaper
for insulation and the UK's first ventilated
photovoltaic array, a method of warm air heating.

Places to Stay – Hotels, Self-Catering & B&Bs

Lubcloud Farm
Oaks in Charnwood, Loughborough,
Leicestershire LE12 9YA
T: +44 (0) 1509 503 204
W: *www.lubcloudfarm.co.uk*
Lubcloud Farm is a small family-run B&B offering
old fashioned hospitality on an organic working
dairy farm. It overlooks the picturesque Vale of
Charley in Charnwood Forest. The farmhouse was
built in the 1800s and has been extended several
times over the centuries. You can still see some of
the original features from the Victorian period in
the hallway namely a row of servant bells,
fireplaces and red and white tile floor. Registered
with the Soil Association.

LINCOLNSHIRE

Places to Eat

The Pink Pig Organic Farm Shop & Restaurant
Holme Hall, Holme, Scunthorpe,
Lincolnshire DN16 3RE
T: +44 (0) 1724 844 466
W: *www.pinkpigorganics.co.uk*
In terms of food miles, Pink Pig Organics is well
placed to enjoy a wealth of local produce, from
Lincoln Red Beef to Lincolnshire Poacher Cheese.

The Soil Association-approved farm also uses its
own produce in many of the hot and cold dishes
served in the 90-seat restaurant.

Places to Visit

The Natural World Centre
Moor Lane, Thorpe on the Hill, Hykeham,
Lincolnshire LN6 9BW
T: +44 (0) 1522 688 868
W: *www.naturalworldcentre.com*
A modern and sustainable visitor centre, the
Natural World Centre offers children an early
insight into eco-friendly living. The permanent
exhibition, Our Changing World, addresses many
21st Century issues affecting the environment,
climate change and the future of the planet. The
exhibitions are interactive and informative and the
Boardwalk Café with stunning lakeside views
contains a wealth of Lincolnshire food. The centre
is located in Whisby Nature Park, a former sand and
gravel quarry which has seen a renaissance during
the past 20 years. Now there are marked pathways
circling lakes, heaths and woodland.

Places to Stay – Hotels, Self-Catering & B&Bs

Poachers Hideaway
Flintwood Farm, Belchford, Horncastle,
Lincolnshire LN9 5QN
T: +44 (0) 1507 533 555
W: *www.poachershideaway.com*
On Flintwood Farm in the Lincolnshire
Wolds you'll find six converted farmhouse
cottages with original features such as
SILVER exposed beams and oak floors. The farm
covers 170 acres of ancient woodland, wildflower
pastures, natural hedgerows and water meadows
so there's plenty of opportunities for walking and
wildlife watching. Permission has also been given
for the building of ten eco-lodges in the grounds
of Flintwood Farm to incorporate rainwater
collection systems and reed-bed treatment of
waste water.

Eco-Lodge Lincolnshire
Rose Cottage, Station Road, Old Leake,
Boston, Lincolnshire PE22 9RF
T: +44 (0) 1205 871 396
W: *www.internationalbusinessschool.net*
Lincolnshire's eco-lodge sprung up among the
cabbage fields and helped usher in a new way to go
green on holiday. The lodge was built using local
wood and its energy sources include a wind turbine
and a wood burning range for heating and hot

water. The outside privy is as luxurious as compost toilets come, stocked with recycled toilet paper, sawdust to toss down the hole and handy back issues of the Dalesman. The outside porch affords a comfortable spot in which to sleep, think or engage in conversation with Andy the Woodsman. **For more insight into ecoscape 25 see pages 74-75.**

NOTTINGHAMSHIRE

Places to Visit

Attenborough Nature Centre
Barton Lane, Attenborough, Nottingham, Nottinghamshire NG9 6DY
T: *+44 (0) 115 972 1777*
W: *www.attenboroughnaturecentre.co.uk*
On the flood plain of the River Trent, one of England's most important waterways, Attenborough Nature Centre is a haven for wildlife. Its busy network of walkways and islands Criss-crosses an open expanse of water. Here sightings of rare Kingfishers and Bitterns are regular occurrences as are the appearance of otters, slowly increasing in numbers. A causeway connects mainland with the visitor centre which opened in 2005. **For more insight into ecoscape 26 see pages 76-77.**

SHROPSHIRE

Places to Eat

Acorn Wholefood Café
26 Sandford Avenue, Church Stretton, Shropshire SY6 6BW
T: *+44 (0) 1694 722 495*
W: *www.wholefoodcafe.co.uk*
The Bland family's restaurant Acorn Wholefood Café is anything but bland. Ingredients are selected and cared-for and dishes are all homemade and wholesome. Fruit is picked locally to go into the nostalgia-inducing pies and jams and organic flour is used for the pastry. The sun-soaked tea garden is a relaxing place to enjoy fairtrade teas and coffees.

Places to Stay – Hotels, Self-Catering & B&Bs

Buckshead Cottage
Brynmawr Farm, Newcastle, Craven Arms, Shropshire SY7 8QU
T: *+44 (0) 1588 640 298*
W: *www.clunvalleyorganics.co.uk*

The Wheelers at Brynmawr Farm turned to organic farming following ill health from crop spray and have admirably transformed their business into a success. Buckshead Cottage, a self-catering property was unoccupied for nearly a century until recent renovation. Electricity and water were introduced to the cottage for the first time using energy from a wind turbine and water from a nearby spring heated by solar panelling on the roof. Guests are permitted to pick organic vegetables growing in the surrounding garden. The cottage enjoys views over the Clun Valley and is close to the Offas Dyke Path, one of 15 national walking trails.

Ecocabin
Langdale Cottage, Obley, Bucknell, Shropshire SY7 0BZ
T: *+44 (0) 1547 530 183*
W: *www.ecocabin.co.uk*
Increasing numbers of ecocabin guests are arriving by bicycle to this little eco-friendly lodge in the Shropshire Hills. The purpose built cabin uses local Douglas Fir wood, sheep's wool for insulation and native ash for flooring. The energy sources come from solar panels for electricity and hot water and wood pellets for the stove. The local economy is benefiting from the 'buy local' shopping service offered by the 'honesty' shop inside the Ecocabin. **For more insight into ecoscape 28 see pages 82-83.**

WARWICKSHIRE

Places to Visit

Garden Organic Ryton
Wolston Lane, Coventry, Warwickshire CV8 3LG
T: *024 7630 3517*
W: *www.gardenorganic.org.uk*
A place to 'eat the view', Garden Organic Ryton is a living demonstration of the importance of organic gardening and shows visitors just how it's done. The aim is to inspire people to eat organic and grow organically at home. The ten acres of landscaped grounds are a riot of colour and smell via wildflower meadows, cornfields and blue seas of lavender. The organic menu in the restaurant serves food – you guessed it – straight from the gardens. It's all homemade and served in full view of the grounds.

WEST MIDLANDS

Places to Eat

Sibila's Restaurant

Canal Square, Browning Street,
Birmingham, West Midlands B16 8EH
T: *+44 (0) 121 456 7634*
W: *www.sibilasrestaurant.co.uk*

The Italo-Croatian chef Sibila Strazicic Cincotti brings you innovative organic vegetarian cuisine. Global influences span from North Africa through the Mediterranean and Turkey to Scandinavia and Northern Europe and come alive in this central Birmingham restaurant. The canal side location shares the same premises as a holistic day spa to continue indulging.

The Warehouse Café

54-57 Allison Street, Digbeth,
Birmingham, West Midlands B5 5TH
T: *+44 (0) 121 633 0261*
W: *www.thewarehousecafe.com*

In the centre of Birmingham, the Warehouse Café is a friendly eatery serving fresh, home-made vegetarian and vegan dishes. Organic peanuts and bulgur wheat go into the home-made veggie burgers and are complimented by thick hand-cut potato wedges. A children's menu ensures the little ones don't go without.

Places to Visit

Birmingham Botanical Gardens

Westbourne Road, Edgbaston, Birmingham,
West Midlands B15 3TR
T: *+44 (0) 121 454 1860*
W: *www.birminghambotanicalgardens.org.uk*

The gardens and glasshouses of Birmingham Botanical Gardens provide a unique setting to get to grips with issues of biodiversity and sustainability. The purpose-built centre on the site holds educational events and workshops including a children's gardening club.

WORCESTERSHIRE

Places to Visit

Bodenham Arboretum and Earth Centre

Wolverley, Kidderminster,
Worcestershire DY11 5SY
T: *+44 (0) 1562 852 444*
W: *www.bodenham-arboretum.co.uk*

On a working farm north of Kidderminster, Bodenham Arboretum is home to over 2,600 species of trees and shrubs, and rich in habitats for wild flowers, water-fowl and other birds. Miles of paths lead visitors through dells, glades, lakes and pools. The visitor centre has won awards for its low impact design carefully tucked into the landscape and topped with a grass roof.

The North of England

Go Full Circle in a Lake District yurt – see page 178

Rare breed sheep at Grindon Cartshed, Northumberland – see page 179

GO SLOW
IN THE NORTH
OF ENGLAND

This vast area made up of Yorkshire, Northumberland, Cumbria, Merseyside and Manchester is best explored slowly. There is the ultimate in slow transportation in the form of the North Yorkshire Moors railway (www.nymr.co.uk) which chugs through the North Yorkshire Moors National Park from Pickering to Grosmont. It's more like a journey back in time to a period when the train was the future of British mass transportation and people enjoyed their journey as much as their destination. Today you can do the same.

SLOW TRAVEL OPTIONS

Travel Dales
W: www.traveldales.org.uk
The Yorkshire Dales National Park is heaving under the pressure of too many cars visiting the area. Travel Dales offers advice to visitors to help them leave the car behind and use the network of public transport options. Travellers by bus are eligible to receive discounts at participating cafés, pubs, B&Bs and other attractions in the Dales.

The Coast to Coast Walk
W: www.wainwright.org.uk
Travel writing legend Arthur Wainwright devised the Coast to Coast walk linking up the North Sea with the Irish Sea passing through the Lake District, Yorkshire Dales, and North Yorkshire Moors. The walk is challenging and at times extreme, but offers incredible sights across world-renowned scenery. West to East the walk starts in St Bees and ends in Robin Hood's Bay.

Stagecoach in the Lake District
W: www.stagecoachbus.com/northwest
When I arrived in the Lake District I was pleased to find that getting around by bus is easy and buses are pretty frequent. In fact catching the bus became a sight-seeing expedition in itself particularly between Windermere and Keswick. Walkers also make use of the buses through Cumbria, hopping on and off as needed. It's affordable and day passes are available.

CHESHIRE

Places to Stay – Hotels, Self-Catering & B&Bs

Harrop Fold Farm
Rainow, Macclesfield, Cheshire SK10 5UU
T: +44 (0) 1625 560 085
W: www.harropfoldfarm.co.uk
Situated conveniently on the Gritstone Trail to the west of the Peak District National Park, Harrop Fold Farm is a family run property which has gained recognition for its environmental policies. Keen to keep the local suppliers busy, the farm maintains a strict low food miles policy and guests can benefit from home reared beef and free range farm eggs. The converted farm buildings contain many original features including antique beds and open fires with accommodation for both self catering and bed and breakfast. The farm also offers residential art courses with their artist in residence.

Places to Stay – Campsites & Holiday Parks

Delamere Touring Park
Station Road, Delamere, Northwich, Cheshire CW8 2HZ
T: +44 (0) 1606 889 231
W: www.campingandcaravanningclub.co.uk
Delamere Park is a family friendly and ecologically sound camping and touring park. Located on the edge of a pine forest, the site has incorporated a number of sustainable features ranging from solar panels to heat the showers to a wood stove to heat the reception area using coppiced wood from the forest. Attractive wild flower meadows have been planted around the site along with 2,500 native deciduous trees.

COUNTY DURHAM

Places to Stay – Hotels, Self-Catering & B&Bs

YHA Langdon Beck
Forest-in-Teesdale, Barnard Castle, County Durham DL12 0XN
T: 0870 770 5910
W: www.yha.org.uk
One of two 'green beacon' YHA hostels, Langdon Beck has incorporated a comprehensive range of environmentally friendly features to accommodate travellers to the North Pennines. As one of the

highest hostels in England, its location is perfect for harnessing renewable wind energy through its turbine. Solar heat photovoltaic installations and wood burning stoves provide further energy sources which have greatly reduced carbon dioxide emissions since their introduction in 2000.

CUMBRIA

Places to Eat

The Jumble Room
Langdale Road, Grasmere, Cumbria LA22 9SU
T: +44 (0) 1539 435 188
W: www.jumbleroom.co.uk
The Jumble Room is a much loved choice for eating frequented by locals and visitors alike. Children are most welcome here, in fact, they helped decorate the place with their cheerful drawings. It's cosy and intimate, and the food is all homemade and organic where possible. The fresh baked walnut and date bread is the perfect partner to the soup of the day. The restaurant is open for lunch and dinner.

Places to Visit

Low Bank Ground Environmental Education Centre
Coniston, Cumbria LA21 8AA
T: +44 (0) 1539 441 314
W: www.lakelandoutdoorcentres.com
Low Bank Ground offers an explosive mix of action and environment on the shores of Coniston Water in the Lake District. The Centre organises activity sessions like sailing and canoeing in the water or mountain biking in Grizedale Forest. Basic accommodation is provided for groups and the Centre hosts themed activities for adults and young people.

Activities

Country Lanes Lake District
The Railway Station, Windermere, Cumbria LA23 1AH
T: +44 (0) 15394 44544
W: www.countrylanes.co.uk
If you take the train to Windermere in the Lake District, Country Lanes offer cycle hire adjacent to the railway station. There are a mix of mountain bikes and hybrids to hire – all in excellent condition. They are available for the day or it's also possible to hire a bike for your entire visit. Their fleet includes bicycles and trailers for children.

Places to Stay – Hotels, Self-Catering & B&Bs

Cumbria House
1 Derwentwater Place, Keswick, Cumbria CA12 4DR
T: +44 (0) 17687 73171
W: www.cumbriahouse.co.uk

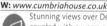

SILVER Stunning views over Derwent Water are coupled with a warm and generous welcome at Cumbria House. A dedicated family effort has turned this bed and breakfast into environmentally friendly guest accommodation with fairtrade breakfasts and a discount for arrivals by public transport. Mavis and Partick, the owners, are also raising money for the Lake District Tourism and Conservation Partnership. For more insight into ecoscape 38 see page 100-101.

Lancrigg Vegetarian Country House Hotel
Easedale, Grasmere, Cumbria LA22 9QN
T: +44 (0) 1539 435 317
W: www.lancrigg.co.uk
The setting very much sells Lancrigg Hotel. It offers a full dose of Wordsworth country with the lakeland mountains, its 30-acres of private grounds and views over the fells. The old 17th Century house has close links with the English poet who spent hours writing in its shadow. Although the rooms can feel a little dated today, the Hotel's restaurant offers adventurous vegetarian cuisine and organic wines.

Moss Grove Organic Hotel
Grasmere, Ambleside, Cumbria LA22 9SW
T: +44 (0) 1539 435 251
W: www.mossgrove.com
Each of the 11 bedrooms at Moss Grove Organic Hotel has its own unique character many with a bold wooden bed and an expanse of elaborate hand screened wallpaper in common. The beds are made from reclaimed timber, sustainable wood sources or natural leather and are complimented by duck down duvets and opulent bathrooms stocked with organic toiletries. For more insight into ecoscape 30 see pages 84-85.

Shankwood Log Cabin
Whitecloserigg, Longtown, Carlisle, Cumbria CA6 5TY
T: +44 (0) 7808 586 950
W: www.fishinghideaway.co.uk
This secluded eco log cabin is hidden in acres of ancient woodland and enjoys a serene two-miles of the River Lyne to catch fish, bathe in rock pools or

explore the surrounding forest by foot. The pools dotted along the stretch of river are all given names such as Otterston, The Deep and Foul Bottom relating to the fish population and visiting wildlife. The cabin has no mains connection but instead is supplied with a peat toilet and solar panelling for lighting and a wood burner for heating. The barbeque is an excellent addition for slow summer evening meals.

Shankwood Log Cabin, Cumbria

Willowford Farm

Gilsland, Cumbria CA8 7AA
T: *+44 (0) 16977 47962*
W: *www.willowford.co.uk*
Close to Hadrian's Wall in Cumbria, Willowford Farm B&B is in a converted farm byre with five immaculately presented rooms. Lauren and Liam, owners of Willowford Farm use local and organic ingredients from their farm to feed their guests. The B&B's heating and hot water is provided by a log-burning boiler using wood from local sawmills and recycling plants as well as bits and pieces from the farm. Lauren and Liam run the farm to Soil Association standards and keep a flock of Swaledale ewes and a hive of bees.

Places to Stay – Campsites & Holiday Parks

Full Circle Lake District Yurts

Rydal Hall, Ambleside, Cumbria LA22 9LX
T: *+44 (0) 1539 821 278*
W: *www.lake-district-yurts.co.uk*
Living without corners, Full Circle is an upmarket camping experience that brings a taste of Mongolia to the Lake District. The yurts are fitted out with lanterns, deep rugs and wood burning stoves. They're not connected to mains anything and so have their own supply of spring water and enjoy nothing but dark starry nights. The position of the yurts at Rydal Hall benefits from great views over Lake Windermere and Loughrigg.

GREATER MANCHESTER

Places to Eat

Eighth Day

111 Oxford Road, All Saints, Manchester, Greater Manchester M1 7DU
T: *+44 (0) 161 273 4878*
W: *www.eighth-day.co.uk*
We've all heard the line: 'on the seventh day, God created Man-chester'. Well on the eighth day, it appears that a vegetarian and vegan healthfood shop came onto the Manchester scene. Actually it was in 1970 during the hey day of hippies and free love. Today Eighth Day is a well-stocked organic shop and bustling café serving veggie breakfast in the morning and healthy lunches at noon.

LANCASHIRE

Places to Stay – Hotels, Self-Catering & B&Bs

Bleasdale Cottages

Lower Fairsnape Farm, Bleasdale, Preston, Lancashire PR3 1UY
T: *+44 (0) 1995 61343*
W: *www.bleasdalecottages.co.uk*
Wildlife enthusiasts get excited about the Forest of Bowland because of its rich diversity of birdlife and landscapes. Amid all this you'll find Bleasdale Cottages – a set of newly converted stone farm buildings. The cottages are completely surrounded by open countryside and feature a wood pellet heating system along with numerous initiatives to reduce waste and energy consumption.

One of the bedrooms at Willowford Farm B&B, Cumbria © Joan Thirlaway

NORTHUMBERLAND

Places to Visit

Alnwick Garden

Denwick Lane, Alnwick,
Northumberland NE66 1YU
T: *+44 (0) 1665 511 350*
W: *www.alnwickgarden.com*

The Duchess of Northumberland had a vision to turn the gardens at Alnwick into a veritable wonderland of grottos, mazes, fountains and a giant tree house. The result is truly inspired. Her Grand Cascade is one of the largest water features in the UK. Water for the fountain is filtered and recycled to minimise waste. The wood for the enormous tree house comes from a sustainable source.

Places to Stay – Hotels, Self-Catering & B&Bs

Grindon Cartshed

Grindon Farm, Haydon Bridge, Hexham,
Northumberland NE47 6NQ
T: *+44 (0) 1434 684 273*
W: *www.grindon-cartshed.co.uk*

On a 600-acre farm within walking distance of Hadrian's Wall, David and Jackie run their farmhouse B&B. The farm **SILVER** is home to a flock of rare and very cute coloured Ryeland sheep. Jackie and David ensure that their farm is managed in an environmentally sound way, and help their guests to reduce their impact by using natural cleaning products, local produce and energy saving initiatives.

Kidlandlee Cottages

Harbottle, Morpeth,
Northumberland NE65 7DA
T: *+44 (0) 1669 650 457*
W: *www.kidlandlee.co.uk*

Known as 'the land of the far horizons', this area of Northumberland offers some remote and secluded spots. That's the type of landscape where you'll find Kidlandlee Cottages perched on the edge of views out to moors, hills and valleys. Both cottages have a homely feel with wood burner and comfy sofas. For more active guests there are facilities for drying wet gear. The cottages are also off-grid and use the power of the wind and sun to generate electricity, along with having their own supply of water.

Noah's Place

31 Main Street, Spittal, Berwick-Upon-Tweed,
Northumberland TD15 1QY
T: *+44 (0) 1289 332 141*
W: *www.noahsplace.co.uk*

Noah's Place is a family-run organic bed and breakfast, owned by Humphrey and Nathalie. The house is in the picturesque spa village of Spittal – just yards from a sandy beach. Breakfast is 100% organic and all the linen is natural and allergy free. B&B guests can enjoy a discount in the organic café attached to Noah's Place serving healthy, light lunches.

Southland Farm Cottages

Southlands Farm, Gunnerton, Hexham,
Northumberland NE48 4EA
T: *+44 (0) 1434 681 464*
W: *www.southlandsfarmcottages.co.uk*

Southlands Farm is home to an idyllic trio of cottages that were once a byre and granary store. Today they're renovated to a high standard and incorporate many earth-friendly features while retaining much of the original character of the buildings. Wood burning stoves and open fires make the cottages a welcome retreat after long walks in the Northumbrian countryside. Hosts Charles and Dee support their local producers and even stock the freezers with locally produced food to purchase. This includes game from the farm which the owners catch themselves.

The Hytte

Bingfield, Hexham, Northumberland NE46 4HR
T: *+44 (0) 1434 672 321*
W: *www.thehytte.com*

This grass-covered accommodation is a Norwegian-inspired self-catering property close to Hadrian's Wall. The traditionally **GOLD** built timber hytte provides comfortable lodging for up to eight people with an open plan living area. The experience wouldn't be complete without a sauna and hot tub which can both be found in a separate wooden cabin, a perfect way to soothe aching muscles overworked in the surrounding countryside. The property has full accessibility and an outside veranda. The owners are keen conservationists and have helped preserve the wildlife around the property. **For more insight into ecoescape 37 see pages 98-99.**

TEES VALLEY

Places to Visit

Nature's World
Ladgate Lane, Acklam, Middlesbrough TS5 7YN
T: +44 (0) 1642 594 895
W: www.naturesworld.org.uk
Nature's World offers an insight into sustainable living and the future of the planet through interactive displays and themed trails. Solar powered talking posts help visitors to navigate their way around the 25-acre site which includes a 400-metre long working model of the River Tees. Follow one of several themed trails around organic and composting gardens, reed beds and children's play areas.

TYNE AND WEAR

Activities

Saddle Skedaddle Biking Holidays
Ouseburn Building, Albion Row, Newcastle Upon Tyne, Tyne and Wear NE6 1LL
T: +44 (0) 191 265 1110
W: www.skedaddle.co.uk
Organising a biking holiday can be a bit daunting. So Saddle Skedaddle decided to help people out and set up both guided and self-guided cycling holidays to suit all range of abilities. They operate all around the globe but have an extensive choice of cycling holidays in the UK which include weekend breaks and longer tours. The company has a strict ethical and environmental policy to ensure the groups of cyclists minimise their impact on communities and the planet.

YORKSHIRE

Places to Eat

Seasons Restaurant
Richmond Station, Richmond, Yorkshire DL10 4LD
T: +44 (0) 1748 825 340
W: www.restaurant-seasons.co.uk
The Tudor-inspired railway station in Richmond closed to passengers in the 1960s but more recently became a new arts centre, cinema, restaurant and space for small-scale artisan food producers. Seasons Restaurant inside the station uses local and seasonal produce with menus on a British theme.

The Balloon Tree
Stamford Bridge Road (A166), Gate Helmsley, York, Yorkshire YO41 1NB
T: +44 (0) 1759 373 023
W: www.theballoontree.co.uk
The number 10 bus from York will take you to the doorstep of the Balloon Tree Farm Shop where the emphasis is on farm 'yards' and not food 'miles'. The produce can be picked from the fields, bought in the shop or tasted in the café, assured that the award winning crops are fresh and flavoursome.

The Millrace
2/4 Commercial Road, Kirkstall, Leeds, Yorkshire LS5 3AQ
T: +44 (0) 113 275 7555
W: www.themillrace-organic.com
In an unexpected location, the Millrace is holding its own with an adventurous and enticing organic menu. Local seasonal availability is the driving force behind this popular eatery which draws inspiration from its Yorkshire surroundings. Children don't miss out with a new organic menu available until 7pm.

Wild Ginger Vegetarian & Vegan Café
Behind The Green House, 5 Station Parade, Harrogate, North Yorkshire HG1 1UF
T: +44 (0) 1423 566 122
W: www.wild-ginger.co.uk
Vegans in Harrogate can rejoice at the homemade fare on offer at Wild Ginger – all meat and dairy free. Lunches consist of imaginatively crafted sandwiches, chutney-filled toasties and good old jacket potatoes. Drinks are organic including wines and beers. The café operates a strict recycling policy and uses biodegradable cleaning products.

Produce on sale at the Balloon Tree, Yorkshire

Places to Visit

Gibson Mill

Hardcastle Crags, Hebden Bridge,
Yorkshire HX7 7AP

T: *+44 (0) 1422 844 518*
W: *www.nationaltrust.org*

Gibson Mill belongs to the National Trust and is both historical and environmental in its aims. The former cotton mill generates its own electricity through the hydro-electric turbines and photovoltaic panels. The surrounding woodland provides biomass fuel for heating and natural spring water trickles down the hill to provide the mill with drinking water. Even the lift is powered by the renewable energy of its human occupants through a series of pulleys and weights. For more insight into ecoscape **35** see pages 94-95.

Places to Stay – Hotels, Self-Catering & B&Bs

La Rosa

Egton, Whitby, Yorkshire

T: *07786 072 866*
W: *www.larosa.co.uk*

La Rosa is a nostalgic camping experience. Each of the vans, trucks and tipis are decked out in trappings from times past in a site in the North Yorkshire Moors National Park. La Rosa is low impact through use of oil lamps and fairy lights and a converted shepherd's hut makes for a first class vintage compost toilet. A reclaimed byre has been turned into the shower block and the site limits its occupancy to avoid overcrowding. For more insight into ecoscape **33** see pages 90-91.

Natural Retreats

Hurgill Road, Richmond, Yorkshire DL10 4SG

T: *+44 (0) 161 242 2970*
W: *www.naturalretreats.com*

The lodges near Richmond in North Yorkshire comprise of ten individual residences. They were constructed using wood from sustainable sources, sedum for the roofs and recycled materials for insulation. The bright interiors benefit from tasteful, yet minimal furnishings enhanced by the influx of natural light through impressive glass frontages. For more insight into ecoscape **36** see page 96-97.

Straw Bale Cabin

Village Farm, Brind, Howden, Goole,
Yorkshire DN14 7LA

T: *+44 (0) 1430 410 662*
W: *www.homegrownhome.co.uk*

A valant family effort resulted in the Straw Bale

The old school house now home to Lockton YHA, Yorkshire

Cabin in East Yorkshire. It's built and insulated with straw and incorporates a host of earth-friendly features like a wind turbine for electricity, 'honesty' shop for local produce and natural indoor toilet. It's also light and comfy with lots of delightful and unexpected additions. Work has commenced on a new straw bale cottage on the same farm. For more insight into ecoscape **34** see pages 92-93.

Titantic Spa

Low Westwood Lane, Linthwaite,
Huddersfield, Yorkshire HD7 5UN

T: *0845 410 3333*
W: *www.titanicspa.co.uk*

Titantic Spa is an ecologically friendly spa in West Yorkshire. It is located in a former textiles mill and uses a combined heat and power unit that takes chippings from trees managed sustainably over a controlled time period. The products used in the spa are all natural and the spa has a bore hole to supply the building with water. For more insight into ecoscape **31** see pages 86 – 87.

YHA Lockton

Old School, Lockton, Pickering,
North Yorkshire YO18 7PY

T: *0870 770 5938*
W: *www.yha.org.uk*

A railway trip back in time will take you to the idyllic hamlet of Lockton on the North Yorkshire Moors where forward thinking environmental sustainability has been top of the agenda for this green youth hostel. The former village school and now renovated hostel uses solar panelling to heat the showers and a sedum roof for insulation. Rainwater is harvested to supply the toilets and customers are encouraged to get behind the building's impressive recycling initiatives. Ideal walking and cycling terrain is just moments away through forests and moorland.

Wales

Irish Sea

Anglesey
Colwyn Bay
Conwy
`42`
Gwynedd
`41`
Aberystwyth
Powys
Ceredigion
Cardigan
Pembrokeshire
`40`
`39`
Carmarthershire
Neath Port Talbot
Swansea
Cardiff

Stay aboard the Aberporth Express in Cardigan with Under the Thatch © Greg Stevenson – see page 184

Wales

Sleep in a tipi in Powys at Eco Retreats – see page 188

GO SLOW IN WALES

Rail journeys in Wales are certainly slow. But taken with a good book and a homemade sandwich there is a huge amount of pleasure to be gained from the passing views. Couple that with some good company – stranger or sputnik – you'll wonder where the time went. Taken in haste, journeys across Wales can be painful. So find that window seat, sit back and put your feet up.

SLOW TRAVEL OPTIONS

Arriva Wales
W: *www.arrivatrainswales.co.uk*
The above said views will invariably be obtained from the window of an Arriva Wales carriage – the main train operator in Wales. The network stretches to the Pembrokeshire coast in the west and Anglesey in the North.

Snowdonia Green Key
W: *www.snowdoniagreenkey.co.uk*
Snowdonia Green Key is an initiative set up to encourage travellers to take public transport around Snowdonia National Park. This includes the Sherpa bus service calling at towns such as Llandudno, Betws-y-Coed, Bethesda, Caernarfon, Porthmadog and Llanberis. The Snowdon Sherpa day ticket allows you to hop on and off the Snowdon Sherpa network as many times as you like.

Pembrokeshire Greenways
W: *www.pembrokeshiregreenways.co.uk*
Pembrokeshire Greenways is encouraging visitors to the National Park to use public transport and bicycles to get around. The website provides details of the coastal bus services which link up to railway stations.

CARMARTHENSHIRE

Places to Visit

National Botanic Gardens of Wales
Llanarthne, Carmarthenshire SA32 8HG
T: *+44 (0) 1558 668 768*
W: *www.gardenofwales.org.uk*
The Botanic gardens are the result of a millenium project which saw restoration of one of the UK's finest estates, a place where a myriad of interconnecting waterways and springs once flowed. Today however, nature has returned to its fullest in the diverse selection of gardens and restored aquatic life where the curious past still peers into present day. The Japanese garden is a fine example of Zen philosophy in the working while the perennially wet bog garden is a magnet for dragonflies and damselflies. The estate itself contains a low intensity organic farm where rare sheep varieties are encouraged to breed. The Great Glasshouse is the centrepiece for the attraction: an enormous glass bubble erupting from the hillside and containing plants from Mediterranean climates around the world.

Pen Pynfarch
Llandysul, Carmarthenshire SA44 4RU
T: *+44 (0) 1559 384 948*
W: *www.penpynfarch.co.uk*
Pen Pynfarch is a rural retreat in South West Wales offering self-catering and B&B accommodation in a cottage. The decor is traditional and uses reclaimed materials and furniture. Logs for heating comes from the surrounding woodland and there's a compost toilet and facilities for recycling. Workshops and courses cover all kinds of subjects involving nature, movement and training.

The glasshouse at the National Botanic Gardens, Carmarthenshire

Heartspring

Hill House, Llansteffan, Carmarthen,
Carmarthenshire SA33 5JG
T: +44 (0) 1267 241 999
W: www.heartspring.co.uk

Heartspring uses its supply of spring water to help bring spiritual and physical rejuvenation to its guests. It's all very natural helped on by Welsh coastal views and use of toxic-free, environmentally-friendly materials and natural paints and varnishes. Individual retreats, mini-breaks and self-catering holidays can also be tailor-made with the optional addition of complementary therapy and teaching sessions such as massage, healing and profound relaxation from local practitioners.

CEREDIGION

Places to Eat

The Treehouse

14 Baker Street, Aberystwyth,
Ceredigion SY23 2EJ
T: +44 (0) 1970 615 791
W: www.treehousewales.co.uk

A one-stop organic shop and restaurant in the heart of Aberystwyth. The restaurant's menu varies throughout the day depending on whether you've come for coffee, lunch or dinner. The ingredients, all from fairly-traded and sustainable sources, are found downstairs in the shop and if they're not fresh they're not in.

Places to Stay – Hotels, Self-Catering & B&Bs

Under the Thatch

Felin Brithdir, Rhydlewis, Llandysul,
Ceredigion SA44 5SN
W: www.underthethatch.co.uk

Sleep in The Aberporth Express – a train carriage dating back to 1905 which found its permanent home on the coastal path of West Wales. This is just one of the many unusual self-catering holidays on offer by Under the Thatch. Cottages, chalets, lodges and caravans are restored to health by the team at Under the Thatch which operates across Wales. They use eco-friendly materials to carry out the renovations and incorporate new technologies like solar panelling to reduce the energy consumption of the holiday rentals. They also source local services and produce wherever

possible and plough all profits back into renovating more historical properties in need of some TLC.

Places to Stay – Campsites & Holiday Parks

Fforest Camp

Fforest farm, Cilgerran, Cardigan,
Ceredigion SA43 2TB
T: +44 (0) 1239 623 633
W: www.coldatnight.co.uk

With all the best bits of camping – the outdoors, campfire, birdsong – combined with a few simple conveniences like pret-à-dormir tents and wooden decking below them, we think Fforest Camp might be onto something. Clusters of varying sized tents blend in with the Welsh landscape and the communal lodge and ammenities have been built with lots of earth-friendly features like wood from local sources, composting toilets and rainwater harvesting. The camp can arrange outdoor activities for guests including sea-kayaking and surfing.

DENBIGHSHIRE

Places to Stay – Hotels, Self-Catering & B&Bs

Hafod Elwy Hall

Bylchau, Denbigh, Denbighshire LL16 5SP
T: +44 (0) 1690 770 345
W: www.hafodelwyhall.co.uk

With views to Snowdonia, Hafod Elwy Hall offers bed and breakfast faithful to its history and setting. Rooms are traditional, historic and memorable transporting guests into a different era. The food served is naturally reared on the owner's farm using traditional methods. A wind turbine supplies much of the Hall's electricity and the wood for the stoves is either from windfall or waste at a local joinery company. Newspaper is shredded for animal bedding and there are various other recycling initiatives.

GLAMORGAN

Places to Stay – Hotels, Self-Catering & B&Bs

Bryn Bettws Log Cabins

Gyfylchi Farm, Pontrhydyfen,
Port Talbot , Glamorgan SA12 9SP
T: +44 (0) 1639 642 040
W: www.brynbettwslogcabins.co.uk

The row of log cabins perched on the hillside at

Bryn Bettws has the pleasant air of a Scandinavian ski resort. With a little less snow in South Wales, the cabins are well suited to mountain bikers who enjoy special lock-up facilities on each of the chalets. The verandas at the front of the cabins are an ideal place to finish the end of an action packed day and to contemplate the stunning view with a cool drink to hand. The cabins have a minimal impact on the surrounding environment and the staff receive training on reducing waste and energy consumption.

GWYNEDD

Places to Eat

Bistro Moelwyn

10 High Street, Blaenau Ffestiniog,
Gwynedd LL41 3DB
T: *+44 (0) 1766 832 358*
W: *www.bistromoelwyn.co.uk*
The bright and cheery Bistro Moelwyn in Snowdonia National Park is a good option for eating out in Blaenau Ffestiniog. There are organic and local options on the menu and the restaurant has made improvements on its environmental performance since refurbishment installing waterless urinals, low energy light bulbs and furniture made from sustainable rubber trees.

Places to Visit

Plas Tan y Bwlch – Snowdonia National Park Study Centre

Maentwrog, Blaenau Ffestiniog,
Gwynedd LL41 3YU
T: *+44 (0) 1766 772 600*
W: *www.plastanybwlch.com*
Snowdonia National Park attracts visitors from afar to explore its mountain ranges and green valleys. Plas Tan y Bwlch is an environmental study centre right at the heart of the national park overlooking the valley of the river Dwyryd. Course participants can learn about the formidable environment that surrounds them through subjects like photography, mountain walking, wildlife, folklore and archaeology. You can even brush up on your Welsh language skills while you're there. Accommodation is provided and there's a bar and gardens to help you relax between lessons.

Places to Stay – Hotels, Self-Catering & B&Bs

Bryn Bella

Lôn Muriau, Betws-y-Coed, Gwynedd LL24 0HD
T: *+44 (0) 1690 710 627*
W: *www.bryn-bella.co.uk*
Bryn Bella is ideally situated to explore Snowdonia National Park and for those who are looking for affordable comfort and a hearty breakfast this accommodation is a wise choice. Mark and Joan are passionate believers in doing their bit to reduce their impact on the environment and supporting the local economy. The rear garden has turned into a miniature eco-system as wildlife flourishes and guests can enjoy the fresh eggs supplied by the stock of hens. There is a shared lounge which doubles as a treasure trove of knowledge on local walking and climbing.

Bryn Elltyd Guest House

Tanygrisiau, Blaenau Ffestiniog,
Gwynedd LL41 3TW
T: *+44 (0) 1766 831 356*
W: *www.accommodation-snowdonia.com*
Bryn Elltyd is located in the stunning Snowdonia National Park making this B&B a great choice for outdoor junkies. Hosts John and Ceilia ensure their business has a small impact on the environment by generating their own energy through solar panelling and using trees from their own land to fuel the fire. **For more insight into ecoescape 42 see pages 108-109.**

Graianfryn Vegetarian Guest House

Penisarwaun, Caernarfon, Gwynedd LL55 3NH
T: *+44 (0) 1286 871 007*
W: *www.fastasleep.me.uk*
Nestled between mountains and the sea, Graianfryn plays host to Snowdonia walkers as well as beach lovers who'll find sandy stretches on nearby Anglesey. Whether you're heading for the summit or the sand, hosts Christine and Alan will ensure you leave after a hearty vegetarian breakfast. If you don't believe me, try the full cooked breakfast with homemade rolls.

PEMBROKESHIRE

Places to Eat

Bench Bar

11 High Street, St Davids,
Pembrokeshire SA62 6SB

T: +44 (0) 1437 721 778

W: www.bench-bar.co.uk

Catering for travellers as well as locals in St Davids, Wales, the Bench has an Italian theme inspired by owner Gianni and his wife Jo. There's a cosy atmosphere and a varied menu including pizzas, pasta and seasonally changing homemade ice-cream. The wine list is well-thought-through and affordable.

Activities

Greenways Holidays

The Old School, Station Road, Narbeth,
Pembrokeshire SA67 7DU

T: +44 (0) 1834 862 107

W: www.greenwaysholidays.com

Leave the car behind and explore the Pembrokeshire countryside by foot or bicycle. Greenways Holidays helps travellers to do just that and will put together a selection of tailor-made tours including routes such as the Pembrokeshire Coast Path, South of the Landsker and the Celtic Trail Cycle Route. Transfers from the station, accommodation and cycle hire are included in the price.

Places to Stay – Hotels, Self-Catering & B&Bs

Clynfyw Farm

Clynfyw, Abercych, Boncath,
Pembrokeshire SA37 0HF

T: +44 (0) 1239 841 676

W: www.clynfyw.co.uk

Clynfyw is a working organic farm and expanse of woodland close to the Pembrokeshire Coast National Park. Guests have a choice of five cottages each with their own character set in the grounds of a Victorian mansion. A reedbed system purifies the waste water from the cottages and a biomass burner heats the buildings using wood pellets and chips. The owners also plant trees annually and have created a sculpture trail through the woods.

Dyffryn Isaf

Llandissilio, Pembrokeshire SA66 7QD

T: +44 (0) 1437 563 657

W: www.pembrokeshire-organic-holidays.co.uk

Dyffryn Isaf is a Soil Association organic smallholding in the quiet rural landscape of Pembrokeshire. Dove Cottage on the farm provides a small but cosy self-catering holiday. Owners Bettina and Stephen can provide produce from the farm including organic vegetables, honey and eggs. Their farming methods are in tune with the surroundings and their fields are all herb-rich permanent pasture divided by ancient hedgerows.

The Old Rectory

Castlemartin, , Pembrokeshire SA71 5HW

T: +44 (0) 1646 661 677

W: www.theoldrectoryweb.com

Emma, the friendly host at the Old Rectory likes to treat her guests to good food and a good night's sleep. She has a choice of bed and breakfast and self-catering accommodation. Her breakfast and supper menus are largely organic using simple and wholesome food. Emma even allows guests to camp in the grounds of the house with easy access to Pembrokeshire sandy beaches.

The Roundhouse

The Druidstone Hotel, Broad Haven,
Haverfordwest, Pembrokeshire SA62 3NE

T: +44 (0) 1437 781 221

W: www.druidstone.co.uk

This former croquet pavilion has undergone a renovation by architect Julian Bishop to transform the outbuilding into a cute octagonal eco-cottage. The grey water toilet not only connects to reed bed drainage but also offers a spectacular storm viewing point. Every inch of the Roundhouse refers back to its original mantra to 'maintain but not increase its relevance in the landscape'. There is a restaurant in the hotel although catering facilities are provided. **For more insight into ecoescape 40 see pages 104-105.**

TYF Eco Hotel & Adventure

Caerfai Road, St Davids,
Pembrokeshire SA62 6QS

T: +44 (0) 1437 721 678

W: www.tyf.com

TYF is an organic hotel on the Pembrokeshire coast in Wales. The hotel offers a host of outdoor activities including coasteering, kayaking and climbing to make the most of this stunning stretch of coast. The hotel is housed in a converted windmill and climbing to the top provides an awe-inspiring 360° view of St Davids Peninsula. Organic food is served in the dining room and the bar has a selection of organic wines and beers. **For more insight into ecoescape 39 see pages 102-103.**

Places to Stay – Campsites & Holiday Parks

Forest Tented Lodges

Marros Camp, Marros, Pembrokeshire

T: *07985 169 101*

W: *www.tentedlodges.co.uk*

Forest Tented Lodges offer a Welsh safari experience inspired by the owner's travels to Kenya. Less tiger and more trees, the site is wonderfully blended into its wooded surroundings which include a diverse selection of newly planted trees. The canvas lodges provide a base from which to explore the Pembrokeshire landscape by bike or foot with tea to your tent in the morning as an added bonus. The solar-powered hot showers mean that the site remains off-grid and has no permanent structures.

POWYS

Places to Eat

The Quarry Café

13 Heol Maengwyn, Machynlleth,
Powys SY20 8EB

T: *+44 (0) 1654 702 624*

W: *www.cat.org.uk*

Part of the Centre for Alternative Technology but situated in the centre of Machynlleth, this whole food café provides healthy vegetarian dishes. The café has been serving up breakfast, lunch and dinner for over 29-years and is run by local foodies passionate about organic and local produce.

Places to Visit

The Centre for Alternative Technology

Llwyngwern Quarry, Pantperthog, Machynlleth,
Powys SY20 9AZ

T: *+44 (0) 1654 705 950*

W: *www.cat.org.uk*

A spectacular water-balanced railway delivers visitors to the CAT site, providing the first stop for those interested in discovering sustainable technologies via interactive hands-on displays. These are continually updated to reflect the changes and needs of a society increasingly aware of the need to adopt sustainable technologies and lifestyles. In the summer months there are guided tours, or individual audio-tours are available. For more insight into ecoescape ▣ see pages 106-107.

Activities

Bicycle Beano Cycling Holidays

Erwood, Builth Wells, Powys LD2 3PQ

T: *+44 (0) 1982 560 471*

W: *www.bicycle-beano.co.uk*

Fuelled by bicycle obsessives, Beano cycle holidays are sociable affairs with up to 28 people joining organised rides in beauty spots of England and Wales. Accommodation is provided in country houses, hostels or organic centres – all serving healthy vegetarian meals. The holidays are organised between May and September and destinations include Snowdonia, Pembrokeshire, Brecon Beacons, the South Downs, and the Vale of the White Horse.

Places to Stay – Hotels, Self-Catering & B&Bs

Aberhyddnant Farm Cottages

Crai, Brecon, Powys LD3 8YS

T: *+44 (0) 1874 636 797*

W: *www.abercottages.co.uk*

These homely cottages are located in the heart of the Brecon Beacons National Park on an organically-run farm. The converted farm buildings were once a dairy shed and hayloft but now offer rustic and sustainable holiday living with home grown oak floors and Welsh pine furniture. Order your organic breakfast box in advance and expect the mother-in-law to be round with a basket full of fresh eggs from the farm. Organic home reared beef and lamb is also available. For a small charge you can bring a fishing rod and spend the day by the Aberhyddnant Pools stocked with a healthy supply of brown trout.

Eco-Cabins at CAT

Centre for Alternative Technology,
Machynlleth, Powys SY20 9AZ

T: *+44 (0) 1654 705 982*

W: *www.cat.org.uk*

The Eco-Cabins are perched on a hillside within the site of the Centre for Alternative Technology. As you may expect the cabins are the epitome of low impact. Electricity is provided by wind, water, solar power and biofuels, and waste water and sewage is filtered through a reed bed sewage system. Each cabin is heated by solar water heating panels and woodstoves. Guests also have free entry into the Centre and there is good food served in the vegetarian restaurant.

*Solar panelling next to the cottages at
Yr Hen Stablau, Powys*

Gwalia Farm

Cemaes, Machynlleth, Powys SY20 9PZ
T: *+44 (0) 1650 511 377*
W: *www.gwaliafarm.co.uk*
You can't buy peace and quiet. But you can certainly find it at the remote Gwalia Farm at the southern edge of Snowdonia National Park. The farm has its own wooded conservation area hiding a sparkly lake where you can have a dip or try out the canoe in the company of friendly dragon flies. Olivia and Harry grow much of their own produce to make homemade jams and serve their guests wholesome vegetarian meals. Bed and breakfast guests can enjoy a roaring open fire in the living room while campers can do the same beneath the stars.

Lasswade Hotel

Station Road, Llanwrtyd Wells, Powys LD5 4RW
T: *+44 (0) 1591 610 515*
W: *www.lasswadehotel.co.uk*
Lasswade is an Edwardian country house hotel which serves organic food to its guests. The hotel is located in Britain's smallest town with a population of 500, and has the added bonus of being at the foothills of the Cambrian mountains. The hotel's restaurant has an AA rosette to its name and serves local delicacies of Welsh Black beef and locally reared Lamb. It has even assisted in the revival of food transportation by train collecting its smoked fish at the local railway station on delivery days.

Trericket Mill Vegetarian Guesthouse, Bunkhouse & Camping

*Trericket Mill, Erwood,
Builth Wells, Powys LD2 3TQ*
T: *+44 (0) 1982 560 312*
W: *www.trericket.co.uk*
Trericket was once a busy corn mill and is now a busy lodging for travellers eager to explore the Brecon Beacons. Accommodation comes in a choice of guesthouse, bunkhouse or camping – all with the option of an immensely satisfying vegetarian breakfast. The Mill's legacy is still apparent particularly in the dining area where guests can enjoy organic breakfast between the 'chutes and shafts' of the old mill. The River Wye is popular with kayakers and canoeists and there are plenty of places to hire equipment or take up lessons.

Yr Hen Stablau

Pantlludw, Machynlleth, Powys SY20 9JR
T: *+44 (0) 1654 703 428*
W: *www.selfcateringcottagewales.co.uk*
Welsh for the Old Stables, Yr Hen Stablau offers guests spotless accommodation in a light, high-beamed building. Both environmentally aware and suitable for disabled visitors, Yr Hen Stablau offers seclusion and escapism in the Dyfi Valley. In preserving the building, the owners have invested a great deal of time and money in restoring original features and adding energy efficient sources such as solar panelling and a wood burning stove using wood from their own land. There are gardens to explore, mountain bike trails to ride and the Centre for Alternative Technology is only an hour's walk away.

Places to Stay – Campsites & Holiday Parks

Eco Retreats

*Plas Einion, Furnace, Machynlleth,
Powys SY20 8PG*
T: *+44 (0) 1654 781 375*
W: *www.ecoretreats.co.uk*
Enjoy some well-being and relaxation over a two night tipi stay in a remote location near to the Dyfi Valley in Wales. If you choose the package deal expect to be pampered with a Reiki treatment session by a qualified practitioner before being led through a meditation session at twilight. The rest of the stay is up to you; if you're feeling active take part in a forest or hill walk and visit the Centre for Alternative Technology, or otherwise simply unwind by the camp fire or in the comforting fibres of the sheepskin rug.

Scotland

Scotland

GO SLOW IN SCOTLAND

The overnight sleeper train to Scotland was excitingly efficient – I hit the sack in London Euston and woke up in Edinburgh. Well – actually, I should have hit the sack when the train withdrew from the station but instead I decided to explore the restaurant car and wine list. So I began the trip in style but woke up with a headache. But it was worth it especially since the trip cost less than £20.

The B&B at East Lochhead, Renfrewshire

SLOW TRAVEL OPTIONS

First Scotrail
W: *www.firstgroup.com/scotrail*

The company behind the overnight sleeper train to Edinburgh, Glasgow and Inverness is First Scotrail. Their staff are friendly and helpful on the train and are happy to introduce first-timers to the wonders of the overnight train. First Scotrail also runs the majority of rail routes across the length and breadth of Scotland some of which pass through stunning scenery like the Inverness to Kyle of Lochalsh line in the northern Highlands.

National Express East Coast
W: *www.nationalexpresseastcoast.com*

The East Coast mainline between London and Edinburgh is a high speed rail route linking up Yorkshire, North East England and Scotland. National Express currently runs the franchise and among its aims for the coming years are to make travel simpler and improve on its environmental responsibility. For me, however, getting to Edinburgh from London in under five hours is pretty fast slow travel. Oh and there's also free wifi all the way there.

Caledonian MacBrayne
W: *www.calmac.co.uk*

The leading ferry operator on Scotland's west coast operates between Arran in the south to Lewis in the north. The ferries link up with rail services at Oban, the gateway to the stunning Western Isles. There are ferry passes if you fancy doing a bit of island hopping.

Scottish City Link
W: *www.citylink.co.uk*

Some remote destinations in Scotland can be reached by coach. Scottish City Link covers over 200 towns and cities across Scotland with over 400 services per day on comfortable, modern coaches. It's reliable and does what it says on the tin.

Cycling in Scotland
W: *www.visitscotland.com/cycling*

Among other tasks, VisitScotland promote cycling around the country. In their view the opportunities to explore the highlands and islands by bicycle are too great to miss. Their website offers ideas for over 150 routes ranging from family rides to extreme mountain biking.

ABERDEEN & GRAMPIAN

Places to Stay – Hotels, Self-Catering & B&Bs

Jenny's Bothy Crofthouse
Dellachuper, Corgarff, Strathdon, Aberdeenshire AB36 8YP
T: *+44 (0) 1975 651 449*
W: *www.jennysbothy.co.uk*

Jenny's Bothy is miles from pretty much anywhere. That's why people come here. The self-catering lodge sleeps up to ten people and offers basic but comfortable accommodation. There's a cosy wood burning stove and immediate access to the wildlife and hills of the Cairn Gorms National Park. The bothy is even available during the winter months when access can become challenging due to snow, so best advice is to wear some skis.

ANGUS & DUNDEE

Places to Eat

Wigmores Restaurant
9 Erskine Lane, Broughty Ferry,
Dundee DD5 1DG
T: *+44 (0) 1382 774 135*
W: *www.wigmoresrestaurant.com*

A little out of Dundee centre, but worth the
journey is Wigmores Restaurant in Broughty Ferry.
The food is unpretentious and reasonably priced,
and the restaurant makes the most of its location
near to the sea serving varied seafood dishes along
with vegetarian and meat courses. There's also an
extensive wine list to compliment.

Places to Stay – Hotels, Self-Catering & B&Bs

Apex City Quay Hotel & Spa
1 West Victoria Dock Road,
Dundee, Angus & Dundee DD1 3JP
T: *+44 (0) 1382 309 309*
W: *www.apexhotels.co.uk*

The Apex City Quay Hotel in Dundee has a
connecting Spa consisting of a swimming
pool, hot tubs, sauna and steam room.
GOLD Here chemicals are kept to a minimum.
The pool uses ozone as a cleaner and the hot tubs
use ultra violet light. Treatment products are 100%
natural and delicious-smelling toiletries are
available in dispensers. **For more insight into
ecoescape 43 see pages 110-111.**

ARGYLL, SOUTHERN
HIGHLANDS & ISLANDS

Activities

Northern Light Charters
Achnacraig, Achindarroch, Duror of Appin,
Argyll PA38 4BS
T: *+44 (0) 1631 740 595*
W: *www.northernlight-uk.com*

Working from Oban, on the beautiful west coast of
Scotland, Northern Light Charters offers wildlife
cruises that combine bird-watching, whale-
watching, island hopping and walking. The
company loves to promote the beauty of the seas
and wildlife of the Hebrides and therefore operates
a strict en17onmental policy to ensure minimal
disturbance is caused. Both boats have been
adapted to run on either wind power or biodiesel.

Places to Stay – Hotels, Self-Catering & B&Bs

Argyll Hotel
Isle of Iona, Argyll PA76 6SJ
T: *+44 (0) 1681 700 334*
W: *www.argyllhoteliona.co.uk*

Located on an island off an island, you
can't get much more secluded than the
mystical Isle of Iona. Whilst you'll need to
GOLD catch two ferries and a bus from the
mainland town of Oban, it will most certainly be
worth the journey when you're greeted with warm
Hebridean hospitality at Argyll Hotel and a roaring
open fire to reduce the chill. The hotel is certified
organic with produce from the garden and meat
from local Highland cattle or Argyll hillside lamb.
The historic hotel is situated on the waterfront,
just a short distance from the ferry landing with
views out to the Isle of Mull.

Stay on the beautiful Isle of Iona at the Argyll Hotel

Balmillig B&B

64B Colquhoun Street, Helensburgh,
Argyll & Bute G84 9JP

T: *+44 (0) 1436 674 922*

W: *www.balmillig.co.uk*

 A cosy B&B near to Loch Lomond in Helensburgh. The rooms are immaculately turned out and feature underfloor heating and comfy beds. Outside there's a quiet spot to sit in the garden which is brimming with wildlife. Solar panels provide much of the B&B's electricity and for breakfast you'll be greeted with a choice of Scottish home cooked food like tattie scones and oatcakes.

Cove Park

Peaton Hill, Cove, Argyll & Bute G84 0PE

T: *+44 (0) 1436 850 123*

W: *www.covepark.org*

Cove Park is a getaway for artists and guests looking for inspiration and quiet. Accommodation comes in eco-friendly 'pods' and 'cubes' overlooking the stunning Loch Lomond. The Cubes are converted shipping containers and the Pods were once part of the set on the BBC's Castaway series. They are both light and modern inside and covered with a sedum roof on top. **For more insight into ecoescape 47 see pages 118-119.**

Glencoe Cottages

Torren, Glencoe, Argyll,
Argyll & Bute PH49 4HX

T: *+44 (0) 1855 811 207*

W: *www.glencoe-cottages.com*

 Deep in the Scottish Glens, the cottages at Glencoe are ideally situated for walking, fishing and even skiing on Scotland's oldest resort. The three detached cottages overlook the River Coe and are surrounded by 50-acres of woodland and mountains abundant in wildlife. A naturally filtered spring provides fresh mountain water to each of the cottages and an under floor heating system uses biomass fuel from sustainable forestry woodchips. The cottages are insulated using recycled newspaper and are equipped with modern facilities and a drying room for adventurers.

Torr Buan House

Ulva Ferry, Isle of Mull PA73 6LY

T: *+44 (0) 1688 500 121*

W: *www.torrbuan.com*

 A regular ferry service to Craignure from mainland Oban runs throughout the year linking up with this wild and inspirational island. David Woodhouse, proprietor of

Torr Buan is known locally as the wildlife expert and offers all weather exploration tours of the island to his guests and independent tourists. The house itself provides a dramatic wildlife viewing point where eagles can often be seen circling ahead and the views out to sea are nothing short of spectacular. The sheep insulated building is cosy even in the depths of a wild Hebridean winter.

AYRESHIRE & ARRAN

Places to Stay – Hotels, Self-Catering & B&Bs

Drumskeoch Farm

Drumskeoch Farm, Pinwherry, Girvan,
Ayreshire KA26 0QB

T: *+44 (0) 1465 841 172*

W: *www.drumskeoch.co.uk*

The farmhouse at Drumskeoch has undergone an organic renovation to offer its guests comfortable and sustainable accommodation with panoramic views over the South West Ayrshire hills. Everything from paint to loo paper is organic and Romi serves up stupendous vegetarian breakfasts. The property has its own water supply and a wood fired back boiler for central heating. The owner's journey to self-sufficiency is a work in progress but nonetheless something of inspiration to the farm's guests. There is a drying room for cyclists and walkers.

East Lochhead House, Cottages and Gardens

Largs Road, East Lochhead, Lochwinnoch,
Renfrewshire PA12 4DX

T: *+44 (0) 1505 842 610*

W: *www.eastlochhead.co.uk*

East Lochhead is a family run farm consisting of self-catering and B&B accommodation. As Scottish advocates of the Slow Food Movement, you will be guaranteed a good hearty breakfast of locally sourced food. Six individual self-catering cottages arranged around a courtyard offer a comfortable and homely stay. Barr Loch to the south provides stunning views. The property has recently been linked up with the National Cycle Network with its own private connecting track.

DUMFRIES & GALLOWAY

Places to Stay – Hotels, Self-Catering & B&Bs

Galloway House Estate
Garlieston, Newton Stewart,
Dumfries & Galloway DG8 8HF
T: *+44 (0) 1988 600 694*
W: *www.gallowayhouseestate.co.uk*
The organically farmed Galloway House Estate contains three stunning holiday cottages restored from former use as stables and gamekeeper properties. The stable cottages share an enclosed garden from which guests can pick their own organic produce. The gamekeeper cottage is an escape from modern life with its off-grid status, acquiring its energy sources from the wind and sun. A wonderful hideaway for two with an attic bedroom and open fire for cosy nights in. The estate is only a short walk away from a clearing with a sandy beach perfect for swimming.

FIFE

Places to Eat

Pillars of Hercules
Falkland Cupar, Fife KY15 7AD
T: *+44 (0) 1337 857 749*
W: *www.pillars.co.uk*
Bruce Bennett is an early disciple of the organic movement and set up his farm in 1983. Today the farm is home to a shop, camp site and buzzing café with an outside veranda. The café serves a variety of yummy homemade cakes and healthy lunches using fresh produce from the farm.

A cottage at Galloway House Estate, Wigtownshire

Places to Visit

Earthship Fife
Kinghorn Loch, Kinghorn, Fife KY3 9YG
T: *+44 (0) 1592 891 884*
W: *www.sci-scotland.org.uk*

GOLD The first Earthship to 'land' in the UK was at this spot in Fife. The concept originated in the USA and involves the construction of self-sufficient and affordable buildings which reduce their impact on the environment. The Earthship is built into the landscape and its walls are made from earth-rammed tyres and aluminium cans. It provides its own heating, electricity, water and sewage treatment. Visitors can learn about sustainable building and have the opportunity to be creative with their waste. **For more insight into ecoescape see pages 124-125.**

The Ecology Centre
Craigenealt, Kinghorn, Fife KY3 9YG
T: *+44 (0) 1592 891 567*
W: *www.cfec.org.uk*
Craigencalt Ecology Centre is an interactive environmental education centre. Here children can go pond-dipping and explore the natural environment surrounding the centre. There are also some spectacular views out to the Firth of Forth over the harbour at Kinghorn and out to Bass Rock in the distance. It is also home to an Earthship (see pages 124-125).

HIGHLANDS

Activities

Cairn Gorm Mountain

Aviemore, Highlands PH22 1RB

T: +44 (0) 1479 861 261

W: *www.cairngormmountain.co.uk*

GOLD

Some of the best skiing in Europe can be found in Scotland. With a good dump of snow, the Cairn Gorms can satisfy skiers of all levels. In Aviemore, Cairngorm Mountain offers some of the best skiing and winter sports adventures in Scotland. The company also operates strict environmental criteria to ensure that this beautiful mountain area is protected.

Dolphin Space Programme

c/o Scottish Natural Heritage,
Fodderty Way, Dingwall Business Park,
Dingwall, Ross-shire IV15 9XB

T: 07921 106 144

W: *www.dolphinspace.org*

The Dolphin Space Programme isn't about sending dolphins to space. Rather it is a wildlife tourism partnership set up to promote the sustainable development of marine wildlife-watching and to ensure that dolphins and other marine animals are given the space they need to carry out their daily lives undisturbed by tourism activities. The Dolphin Space Programme is based in the North East of Scotland, an area which is also home to the only resident population of bottlenose dolphins in the North Sea. The Programme dishes out accreditations to cruise operators who agree to observe certain codes of behaviour. The website gives details about all the accredited tour operators.

Places to Visit

Findhorn Foundation

The Park, Findhorn, Forres,
Morayshire IV36 3TZ

T: +44 (0) 1309 690 311

W: *www.findhorn.org*

Findhorn is a spiritual community, ecovillage and educational centre in the North of Scotland. The Community was founded in 1962 and offers a full calendar of holistic education courses plus special events, attracting visitors from all over the world. Visitors are welcome to join guided tours of innovative eco buildings, a water treatment facility, windmills, pottery, weaving and art studios. **For more insight into ecoscape 48 see pages 120-121.**

Places to Stay – Hotels, Self-Catering & B&Bs

Hiddenglen Holidays

Laikenbuie, Grantown Road, Nairn,
Highlands IV12 5QN

T: +44 (0) 1667 454 630

W: *www.hiddenglen.co.uk*

Peter and Therese, owners of Laikenbuie Farm and Hiddenglen Holidays, offer guests a choice of high-end lodges, chalet and caravan accommodation with outlooks over a trout loch and native woods in the wilds of North Scotland. The farm is organic and welcomes WWOOF participants to help out. The lodges are suitable for disabled travellers and are well insulated with south facing living areas.

Loch Ossian Youth Hostel

Corrour, Fort William, Highlands PH30 4AA

T: 0870 004 1139

W: *www.syha.org.uk*

GOLD

Loch Ossian Hostel is as remote as accommodation comes and can only be accessed by foot from the rail station. The hostel's recent renovation has displayed a reverence toward its fragile natural surroundings and encompasses a host of ecological techniques. To protect the bat colony in the attic, water based paint has been used throughout. The hostel was formerly a boathouse and is now familiar among seasoned Munro-baggers. **For more insight into ecoscape 49 see pages 122-123.**

The Cross at Kinguissie

Tweed Mill Brae, Ardbroilach Road, Kingussie,
Highlands PH21 1LB

T: +44 (0) 1540 661 166

W: *www.thecross.co.uk*

SILVER

In a former tweed mill, The Cross has developed its reputation as both an excellent restaurant and a temptation for diners to make a night of it and stay in one of its individually appointed rooms after a dram or two of whisky. The menu changes daily depending on seasons and local availability. **For more insight into ecoscape 46 see pages 116-117.**

Places to Stay – Campsites & Holiday Parks

Rhanich Farm

Edderton, Tain, Ross Shire IV19 1LG

T: +44 (0) 1862 821 265

Big sheep fans, the owners of organic Rhanich Farm have an extensive flock of many different breeds for production of wool, cheese and yoghurt. Lucky campers on the farm can benefit from supplies of homemade breads, chutneys and organic fruit and vegetables.

ISLE OF SKYE

Places to Eat

The Three Chimneys Restaurant with Rooms

Colbost, by Dunvegan, Isle of Skye IV55 8ZT
T: *+44 (0) 1470 511 258*
W: *www.threechimneys.co.uk*
On a remote corner of the Isle of Skye, The Three Chimneys Restaurant serves food influenced by Scotland's culinary heritage. The rugged shoreline of Loch Dunvegan is a perfect setting for this cottage restaurant not least when you enter its cosy interior with low-beamed ceilings, stone walls and an open fire. Seafood and white fish are hauled in from nearby waters and Skye lamb and Highlander beef are reared locally. The accompanying accommodation in The House Over By, features rooms with views and luxurious bedding.

Places to Visit

Rubha Phoil Forest Garden

Armadale Pier, Isle of Skye IV45 8RS
T: *+44 (0) 1471 844 700*
W: *www.skye-permaculture.org.uk*
On the Isle of Skye, Rubha Phoil is a permaculture centre, forest garden and woodland walk. Even the greenest of green fingers can learn a thing or two here. Visitors can explore the certified organic herb gardens and take part in seminars, workshops and demonstration projects. The centre also looks at sustainable design in buildings.

Skye Environmental Centre

7 Black Park, Broadford, Isle of Skye IV49 9DE
T: *+44 (0) 1471 822 487*
W: *www.otter.org*
A registered charity focusing on practical conservation through education and hands-on involvement. The centre runs a wildlife hospital treating all wildlife casualties but specialising in otters. Educational courses are run mainly in the Hebrides for children, adults, students and special courses can be tailor-made for particular groups.

LOTHIAN

Places to Eat

Iglu Ethical Eatery

2b Jamaica Street, Edinburgh, Lothian EH3 6HH
T: *+44 (0) 131 476 5333*
W: *www.theiglu.com*
Food at the Iglu explores wild, organic and Scottish produced ingredients. Charlie Cornelius, the restaurant's owner is passionate about nutritious and ecologically sound food. He serves fish, seafood, game and vegetarian options with an extensive list of organic wines and beers.

Dessert at the Iglu, Edinburgh

Places to Visit

Four Winds Inspiration Centre

The Pavilion, Inverleith Park, Arboretum Place, Edinburgh, Lothian EH3 5NY
T: *+44 (0) 131 332 2229*
W: *www.four-winds.org.uk*
Established in 1998, Four Winds Inspiration Centre is an environmental education and craft-based charity. Situated in an attractive setting within Inverleith Park, Edinburgh, Four Winds provides an opportunity to connect with nature, yourself and others whilst learning new skills and knowledge by participating in the wide range of crafts, herbal and renewable energy courses. Visits are by arrangement.

SCOTLAND

Our Dynamic Earth

112 Holyrood Road, Edinburgh,
Lothian EH8 8AS

T: *+44 (0) 131 550 7800*
W: *www.dynamicearth.co.uk*

Our Dynamic Earth tells an interactive story of the planet – past and present. Visitors travel through space and time to get to grips with the wonders and challenges facing the Earth today and how decisions are made that affect its future.

Find out about Our Dynamic Earth in Edinbugh

Scottish Seabird Centre

The Harbour, North Berwick, Lothian EH39 4SS

T: *+44 (0) 1620 890 202*
W: *www.seabird.org*

 Balanced on a rocky platform jutting out to sea, the Seabird Centre in North Berwick provides a unique wildlife viewing point toward the islands of the Firth of Forth. Visitors can enjoy a privileged insider peak at birdlife and sea creatures of the islands using unobtrusive and state-of-the-art cameras. The live action cameras are fully controllable from the centre and open up unparalleled detail into wildlife behaviour throughout the year. **For more insight into ecoescape** ■ **see pages 112-113.**

Activities

Wild in Scotland

2b Jamaica Street, Edinburgh, Lothian EH3 6HH

T: *+44 (0) 131 476 5333*
W: *www.wildinscotland.com*

Environmentally-sound Wild in Scotland tours help travellers explore the Highlands and Islands of Scotland. The tours begin in Edinburgh and are always in small groups. They operate a budget

friendly kitty system which means that communal living comes with the experience. Wild in Scotland ensures that the local communities benefit from the respectful influx of visitors and that the environment is not harmed in the process. Activities include visiting distilleries, swimming in lochs, hearing the legends of warriors and faeries and seeing some of the UK's most spectacular scenery.

Places to Stay – Hotels, Self-Catering & B&Bs

Apex City Hotel Edinburgh

61 Grassmarket, Edinburgh, Lothian EH1 2JF

T: *+44 (0) 131 243 3456*
W: *www.apexhotels.co.uk*

 The sister hotel to the Apex City of London, the Edinburgh hotel has all the chic and even more of the charm of its counterpart. In the heart of the city with views of Edinburgh Castle, the hotel is famed among business and pleasure seekers alike. The Heights Restaurant looks out to the castle and offers a menu of fine Scottish cuisine. The hotel's commitment to reduce and recycle has been commended and the hotel chain chooses only city locations to avoid building on Greenfield sites. The hotel has supported a local community garden called Heriot Bridge winning third place in the Keep Edinburgh Growing competition.

Ashdene House

23 Fountainhall Road, Edinburgh,
Lothian EH9 2LN

T: *+44 (0) 131 667 6026*
W: *www.ashdenehouse.com*

 A gold award winner in the Green Tourism Business Scheme, Ashdene House is an affordable B&B option just outside Edinburgh city centre. The breakfast menu consists of local meats and my favourite, the vegetarian haggis. The rooms are clean and comfy.

Cluaran House

47 Leamington Terrace, Edinburgh,
Lothian EH10 4JS

T: *+44 (0) 131 221 0047*
W: *www.cluaran-house-edinburgh.co.uk*

Cluaran House is a large terraced Victorian home dating from the 1860's. The property has been completely renovated and redecorated in bright, harmonious colours to compliment its airy, spacious interior. Organic food is served for breakfast with vegetarian and vegan options available.

Eildon Bed and Breakfast

Eildon House, 109 Newbigging, Musselburgh, Edinburgh, Lothian EH21 7AS

T: *+44 (0) 131 665 3981*

W: *www.stayinscotland.net*

Eildon House is a listed Georgian building dating back to the 1800's. The present owner Eve has sympathetically restored it **GOLD** from its derelict state over the last decade and now welcomes guests to stay. Eve has implemented lots of small energy and waste saving initiatives throughout the B&B and uses fresh locally sourced produce whenever she can.

Radisson SAS Hotel Edinburgh

80 High Street, The Royal Mile, Edinburgh, Lothian EH1 1TH

T: *+44 (0) 131 557 9797*

W: *www.edinburgh.radissonsas.com*

The rooms at the Radisson in Edinburgh are modern and spacious. You'll find stocks of fairtrade tea and coffee along with organic **GOLD** fruit and locally sourced snacks and water. Housekeeping staff are trained in ensuring that towels are only cleaned when necessary and recycling is maintained wherever possible. Each year the staff vote for a local charity to support and have a say in community initiatives. **For more insight into ecoescape** 45 **see pages 114-115.**

ORKNEY

Places to Stay – Hotels, Self-Catering & B&Bs

Woodwick House

Evie, Orkney KW17 2PQ

T: *+44 (0) 1856 751 330*

W: *www.woodwickhouse.co.uk*

This hotel on a sheltered spot of the Orkney Isles is set among twelve acres of bluebell woodland. It even has its own private bay – a great place to watch for seals and other wildlife. Evening meals are prepared from the wealth of local Orkney produce and are organic where possible. Local artists have helped decorate the walls and there's an open fire in the sitting room for chilly evenings.

Trumland Farm

Rousay, Orkney, Orkney Islands KW17 2PU

T: *+44 (0) 1856 821 252*

On a working organic farm, Trumland consists of a hostel, campsite and self-catering cottage. It's warm, clean and affordable, and crucially, situated on the stunning Island of Rousay in the Orkney Isles. People come here for the wildlife – otters, seals and birds – and to explore the wildness of the scenery.

SCOTLAND

PERTHSHIRE

Places to Eat

Jamesfield Organic Centre

Jamesfield Farm, Abernethy, Perthshire KY14 6EW

T: *+44 (0) 1738 850 498*

W: *www.jamesfieldfarm.co.uk*

Brothers Roy and Ian run the organic farm and Centre at Jamesfield, a fine example of connecting producer with consumer. As well as a reputable selection of organic meats from the farm, the centre contains a restaurant, butchery, bakery and farm shop. With so much produce available from the farm, food miles are clearly not an issue.

Places to Stay – Hotels, Self-Catering & B&Bs

Duncrievie Log Cabins

Hilton of Duncrievie Farm, Glenfarg, Perth, Perthshire PH2 9PD

T: *08705 342342*

W: *www.hoseasons.co.uk*

The trio of log cabins on Duncrievie Farm are heated with ground source heat pumps and feature hot tubs and saunas. The **GOLD** meadows of the organic farm setting encourage wildlife, and guests can enjoy walks from the door over Ochil Hills and the Lomond Hills of Fife.

GLASGOW & CLYDE VALLEY

Places to Eat

Tapa

19-21 Whitehill Street, Dennistoun, Glasgow, Strathclyde G31 2LH

T: *+44 (0) 141 554 9981*

W: *www.tapabakehouse.co.uk*

Freshly roasted coffee and oven fresh bread are the specialities served at Tapa in Glasgow. Everything is organic including the irresistible selection of home baked cakes and biscuits. An organic breakfast is available almost every morning and soups, sandwiches and salads are available throughout the day.

Index

Acknowledgements

The one person I'd like to thank more than anyone in the world is Andy. He's been there throughout these exciting and challenging times and is always full of support and kindness. I couldn't have done it without him.

Next thank you to Mum and Dad, who've promoted my guide to everyone they meet which has been a great help when it's been most needed. Of course, thank you to Gavin, the publisher who's taken on a new project and opened himself up to the world of travel. I hope he's enjoying it.

So to the other wonderful people who have been part of the new ecoescape guide:

Adam Vaughan
Alexandra Hammond
Al Tepper
Arabella Stewart
Barbara Basford
Bernice Markham
Catherine Mack
Chris Greenman
Deborah Benham
Ed Gillespie
Ed Veasey
Emily Blunden
Faith Johnson
Freda Palmer
Geri Clarke
Gill Jenkins

Giovanna Dunmall
Helga Pearson
Howard Vaughan
Jamie Andrews
Jez Swinscoe
Jo Harbisher
John Lyle
Jonty Whittleton
Kash Bhattacharya
Laura Lawson
Liz Hingley
Luke Rowlands
Lynsey Fletcher
Mark Smith
Matthew Rawlingson
Plant

Mod Le Froy
Neil Warren
Oliver Beard
Omaid Hiwaizi
Penney Poyzer
Rhiannon Batten
Richard Hammond
Rosie Inge
Sarah Loftus
Shirley Greenman
Simon Brown
Stasa Veroukis
Tara Basnet
Thea Atkinson-Holmes
Thomas Heath
Victoria Peat

Thanks to all the retailers that had faith in ecoescape and stocked the first edition in their stores

Get more ecoescapes . . .

Copies of our books and guides can be purchased online at
www.greenguide.co.uk or you can usually find them in bookshops,
independent retailers and organic and wholefood stores. If you need help
finding a local store stocking our books please call us on +44 (0) 1945 461 452
or email the publisher via **publisher@greenguide.co.uk**

Our titles include:

ecoescapes

ecoescape: United Kingdom £8.99
ISBN: 978-1-905731-40-4

ecoescape: Ireland (May 2008) £8.99
ISBN: 978-1-905731-29-9

ecoescape: British Islands (September 2008) £8.99
ISBN: 978-1-905731-29-9

ecoescape: Budgets & Backpackers (September 2008) £8.99
ISBN: 978-1-905731-41-1

Green Guide – *the directory for planet-friendly living*
The Green Guide is a series of books and directories focusing on green and
natural products, services and organisations, supported by a comprehensive website and
occasional magazine. Find out more at www.greenguide.co.uk

Green Guide Essentials £6.99
ISBN: 978-1-905731-01-5

The Green Guide to a Greener Wedding (May 2008) £8.99
ISBN: 978-1-905731-49-7

The Green Guide for London 2008 (May 2008) £12.99
ISBN: 978-1-905731-31-2

The Green Guide to a Greener Home (June 2008) £8.99
ISBN: 978-1-905731-50-3

The Green Guide for Scotland (June 2008) £12.99
ISBN: 978-1-905731-32-9

The Green Guide for Wales (June 2008) £12.99
ISBN: 978-1-905731-36-7

You can also find the Pocket Green Guides for England, Scotland
and Wales on the website.

For retailers & wholesalers
Our books are distributed by **Vine House Distribution Ltd**
The Old Mill House, Mill Lane, Uckfield, East Sussex TN22 5AA
t: +44 (0) 1825 767 396
e: sales@vinehouseuk.co.uk

Responsible escapism notes

Send us your story and inspire others to go green

tellyourstory@ecoescape.org *and* **www.ecoescape.org**

Responsible escapism notes

e: tellyourstory@ecoescape.org
w: www.ecoescape.org

Responsible escapism notes

e: tellyourstory@ecoescape.org
w: www.ecoescape.org

Responsible escapism notes

e: tellyourstory@ecoescape.org
w: www.ecoescape.org

Responsible escapism notes

e: tellyourstory@ecoescape.org
w: www.ecoescape.org